How to develop and implement a national drug policy

Second edition. Updates and replaces
Guidelines for Developing National Drug Policies, 1988

World Health Organization
Geneva

WHO Library Cataloguing-in-Publication Data

How to develop and implement a national drug policy. — 2nd ed.
Updates and replaces: Guidelines for developing national drug policies (1988).

1. Essential drugs – standards   2. Drug and narcotic control
3. Drug utilization – standards   4. Legislation, Drug   5. Guidelines

ISBN 92 4 154547 X   (NLM classification: QV 704)

The World Health Organization welcomes requests for permission to reproduce or translate its publications in part or in full. Applications and enquiries should be addressed to the Office of Publications, World Health Organization, Geneva, Switzerland, which will be glad to provide the latest information on any changes made to the text, plans for new editions, and reprints and translations already available.

The designations employed and the presentation of the material in this publication do not imply the expression of any opinion whatsoever on the part of the Secretariat of the World Health Organization concerning the legal status of any country, territory, city or area or of its authorities, or concerning the delimitation of its frontiers or boundaries.

The mention of specific companies or of certain manufacturers' products does not imply that they are endorsed or recommended by the World Health Organization in preference to others of a similar nature that are not mentioned. Errors and omissions excepted, the names of proprietary products are distinguished by initial capital letters.

Printed in Malta

Contents

Contributors

These guidelines were developed through a series of activities. In June 1995 a meeting of the WHO Expert Committee on National Drug Policy was held, to update the 1988 *Guidelines for Developing National Drug Policies.*[1] Comments and contributions on successive drafts were received from international groups, organizations and individual experts, as well as from staff members from the Department of Essential Drugs and Medicines Policy (EDM) and WHO Regional Offices. The final text was edited by C. Hodgkin, E.D. Carandang, D.A. Fresle and H.V. Hogerzeil.

The comments and contributions of the following persons are gratefully acknowledged: F.S. Antezana, H. Bale, W. Bannenberg, K. Bremer, P. Brudon, J. Cohen, M. Cone, A. Creese, A.W. Davidson, T. Eriksen, M. Everard, M. Fofana, B.B. Gaitonde, G. Gizaw, V. Habiyambere, M. Helling-Borda, D. Henry, K. Hurst, B. Joldal, K. de Joncheere, Kin Shein, Q. Kintanar, S. Kopp-Kubel, R.O. Laing, R.F. Lobo, Y. Maruyama, B. Merkel, M.Murray, S.Muziki, S.Nightingale, T.L.Paal, M.Paz-Zamora, J.D.Quick, L. Rägo, C. Rambert, J.A. Reinstein, H. Rouppe van der Voort, L.B. Rowsell, G. Sitbon, S. Soesilo, P. Spivey, G. Tomson, A. Toumi, G. Velasquez, C. Voumard, K. Weerasuriya, E. Wondemagegnehu and X. Zhang.

Abbreviations and acronyms

AIDS	Acquired immunodeficiency syndrome
ASEAN	Association of South-East Asian Nations
DRA	Drug regulatory authority
EDM	Department of Essential Drugs and Medicines Policy
EU	European Union
GMP	Good manufacturing practices
HIV	Human immunodeficiency virus
INN	International nonproprietary names
INRUD	International Network for Rational Use of Drugs
MoH	Ministry of Health
MSF	Médecins Sans Frontières
MSH	Management Sciences for Health
NDP	National drug policy
NGO	Nongovernmental organization
OAU	Organization of African Unity
OTC	Over-the-counter (drug)
TRIPS	(Agreement on) Trade-Related Aspects of Intellectual Property Rights
TFHE	Task Force on Health Economics
UNAIDS	Joint United Nations Programme on HIV/AIDS
UNICEF	United Nations Children's Fund
UNFPA	United Nations Population Fund
WHA	World Health Assembly
WHO	World Health Organization
WTO	World Trade Organization

Preface

In 1975, the World Health Assembly in resolution WHA28.66 requested WHO to develop means to assist Member States in formulating national drug policies. It also urged WHO to assist countries in implementing strategies, such as the selection of essential drugs and appropriate procurement of quality drugs based on health needs, and in providing education and training in various elements of pharmaceutical programmes. This resolution was followed by a series of events that marked the evolution of country drug programmes with the assistance of WHO.

The first WHO Model List of Essential Drugs was published in 1977. A year later the WHO/UNICEF Conference on Primary Health Care at Alma-Ata included access to essential drugs as one of the eight elements of primary health care. In 1979, the WHO Action Programme on Essential Drugs was established. Another landmark in promoting strategies to improve the pharmaceutical situation in countries was the 1985 Conference of Experts on Rational Use of Drugs in Nairobi. The following year's World Health Assembly adopted resolutions that reflected the Conference recommendations on promoting rational use. Also in 1986, a WHO Expert Committee on National Drug Policies met to develop practical guidance for Member States, published as *Guidelines for developing national drug policies*.[1] This publication has proved very useful over the years.

The efforts of countries, WHO and other agencies have had a considerable impact. The number of people with access to essential drugs has grown from roughly 2,100 million in 1977 to an estimated 3,800 million in 1999. By 1999, 66 countries had formulated or updated a national drug policy within the previous 10 years, compared with 14 countries in 1989. By the end of 1999, 156 WHO Member States had a national essential drugs list; 127 of the lists had been revised within the previous five years.[2]

Nevertheless, problems of access to quality drugs and rational use persist. Although few hard data are available, it is likely that in the poorest parts of Africa and Asia more than half the population still lacks access to essential drugs. And there are new challenges that may have an impact on access, such as the expansion of the private sector's role in pharmaceuticals, health sector reforms and the effects of globalization. The changing pattern of diseases, antimicrobial resistance and emerging new diseases are other factors. Particularly important is the current trend of governments to reduce health care spending because of inadequate resources, despite increasing health needs.

After a decade, and with new problems to be addressed, there was a clear need to revise the 1988 guidelines. The Expert Committee on National Drug Policies met in 1995 to review the current pharmaceutical situation and to start the updating process. Their deliberations resulted in a report that became the basis of the present guidelines.[3]

These updated guidelines focus on the national drug policy process, strategies and options which can be used by Member States and organizations active in the pharmaceutical sector. Each policy component is discussed, with a focus on current problems and new challenges. And each chapter presents strategies and practical approaches that can be used to improve the situation. All chapters include references to publications that provide additional technical and practical details.

PART ONE

How to develop and implement a national drug policy

1 Introduction

1.1 Essential drugs are not used to their full potential

Health is a fundamental human right. Access to health care, which includes access to essential drugs, is a prerequisite for realizing that right. Essential drugs play a crucial role in many aspects of health care. If available, affordable, of good quality and properly used, drugs can offer a simple, cost-effective answer to many health problems. In many countries drug costs account for a large share of the total health budget. Despite the obvious medical and economic importance of drugs there are still widespread problems with lack of access, poor quality, irrational use and waste. In many settings essential drugs are not used to their full potential.

Lack of access to essential drugs

An increasing number of pharmaceutical products are available in the world market, and there has been rapid growth in both drug consumption and expenditure. However, many people throughout the world cannot obtain the drugs they need, either because they are not available or too expensive, or because there are no adequate facilities or trained professionals to prescribe them. Although hard data are unavailable, WHO has estimated that at least one-third of the world's population lacks access to essential drugs; in poorer areas of Asia and Africa this figure may be as high as one-half.[2] Millions of children and adults die each year from diseases that could have been prevented or treated with cost-effective and inexpensive essential drugs.

Poor quality

In many countries drug quality assurance systems are inadequate because they lack the necessary components. These components include adequate drug legislation and regulations, and a functioning drug regulatory authority with adequate resources and infrastructure to enforce the legislation and regulations. Without these, substandard and counterfeit products can circulate freely. In addition, inappropriate handling, storage and distribution can alter the quality of drugs. All these factors may have serious health consequences and lead to a waste of resources.

Irrational use of drugs

Even people who have access to drugs may not receive the right medicine in the right dosage when they need it. Many people buy, or are prescribed and dispensed, drugs that are not appropriate for their needs. Some use several drugs when one would do. Others use drugs that carry unnecessary risks. The irrational use of drugs may unnecessarily prolong or even cause ill-health and suffering, and results in a waste of limited resources.

Persistent problems and new challenges

These problems have persisted despite all the work done to improve access to essential drugs, to ensure drug quality and to promote rational drug use. The reasons are complex and go beyond simple financial constraints. To understand them it is necessary to look at the characteristics of the drug market, and to study the attitudes and behaviour of governments, prescribers, dispensers, consumers and the drug industry. Health sector development, economic reform, structural adjustment policies, trends towards liberalization, and new global trade agreements all have a potential impact on the pharmaceutical situation in many countries. They may also affect the ultimate goal of achieving equity in health.

Changes in the patterns of disease and drug demand also represent major challenges. The rise of new diseases, such as acquired immunodeficiency syndrome (AIDS), the re-emergence of other diseases and increasing drug resistance of potentially fatal diseases, such as malaria and tuberculosis, all contribute to increased spending on drugs and growing pressure on health resources. Changes in life expectancy and in lifestyles have led to an increase in chronic diseases and diseases of the elderly, and an increase in the need for drugs to treat these chronic diseases.

A national drug policy as a common framework to solve problems in pharmaceuticals

Experience in many countries has shown that these complicated and interdependent problems can best be addressed within a common framework, as piecemeal approaches can leave important problems unsolved and often fail. In addition, the different policy objectives are sometimes contradictory, and so are the interests of some of the stakeholders. On the basis of this experience, WHO recommends that all countries formulate and implement a comprehensive national drug policy (NDP).

1.2 What is a national drug policy?

A commitment to a goal and a guide for action

A national drug policy is a commitment to a goal and a guide for action. It expresses and prioritizes the medium- to long-term goals set by the government for the pharmaceutical sector, and identifies the main strategies for attaining them. It provides a framework within which the activities of the pharmaceutical sector can be coordinated. It covers both the public and the private sectors, and involves all the main actors in the pharmaceutical field.

A national drug policy, presented and printed as an official government statement, is important because it acts as a formal record of aspirations, aims, decisions and commitments. Without such a formal policy document there may be no general overview of what is needed; as a result, some government measures may conflict with others, because the various goals and responsibilities are not clearly defined and understood.

The policy document should be developed through a systematic process of consultation with all interested parties. In this process the objectives must be defined, priorities must be set, strategies must be developed and commitment must be built.

Why is a national drug policy needed?

A national drug policy is needed for many reasons. The most important are:

- to present a formal record of values, aspirations, aims, decisions and medium- to long-term government commitments;

- to define the national goals and objectives for the pharmaceutical sector, and set priorities;

- to identify the strategies needed to meet those objectives, and identify the various actors responsible for implementing the main components of the policy;

- to create a forum for national discussions on these issues.

The consultations and national discussions preceding the drug policy document are very important, as they create a mechanism to bring all parties together and achieve a sense of collective ownership of the final policy. This is crucial in view of the national effort that will later be necessary to implement the policy. The policy *process* is just as important as the policy *document*.

The main objectives of ensuring equitable access, good quality and rational use are usually found in all national drug policies, but clearly not all of these policies are the same. The final definition of objectives and strategies depends on the level of economic development and resources, on cultural and historical factors, and on political values and choices. The guidelines set out here are intended to help countries develop and implement a comprehensive policy framework that is appropriate to their own needs, priorities and resources.

A national drug policy is an essential part of health policy

A national drug policy cannot be developed in a vacuum – it must fit within the framework of a particular health care system, a national health policy and, perhaps, a programme of health sector reform. The goals of the national drug policy should always be consistent with broader health objectives, and policy implementation should help to achieve those broader objectives.

The health policy and the level of service provision in a particular country are important determinants of drug policy and define the range of choices and options. On the other hand, the drug situation also affects the way in which health services are regarded. Services lose their credibility if there is no adequate supply of good quality drugs, or if these are badly prescribed. Thus the implementation of an effective drug policy promotes confidence in and use of health services.

There are also economic arguments. In many countries a large proportion of health care spending is on drugs. Health care financing is therefore closely related to drug financing. It is very difficult to implement a health policy without a drug policy.

Objectives of a national drug policy

In the broadest sense a national drug policy should promote equity and sustainability of the pharmaceutical sector.

The general objectives of a national drug policy are to ensure:

- Access: equitable availability and affordability of essential drugs
- Quality: the quality, safety and efficacy of all medicines
- Rational use: the promotion of therapeutically sound and cost-effective use of drugs by health professionals and consumers.

The more specific goals and objectives of a national policy will depend upon the country situation, the national health policy, and political priorities set by the government. In addition to health-related goals there may be others, such as economic goals. For example, an additional objective may be to increase national pharmaceutical production capacity.

It is critical that all the drug policy's objectives are explicit, so that the roles of the public and private sectors and of the various ministries (health, finance, trade and industry) and government bodies (such as the drug regulatory authority) can be specified.

Importance of the essential drugs concept

The essential drugs concept is central to a national drug policy because it promotes equity and helps to set priorities for the health care system. The core of the concept is that use of a limited number of carefully selected drugs based on agreed clinical guidelines leads to a better supply of drugs, to more rational prescribing and to lower costs.

The reasons are clear. Essential drugs, which are selected on the basis of safe and cost-effective clinical guidelines, give better quality of care and better value for money. The procurement of fewer items in larger quantities results in more price competition and economies of scale. Quality assurance, procurement, storage, distribution and dispensing are all easier with a reduced number of drugs. Training of health workers and drug information in general can be more focused, and prescribers gain more experience with fewer drugs and are more likely to recognize drug interactions and adverse reactions.

By the end of 1999, 156 developed and developing countries had national or institutional lists of essential drugs for different levels of care, in both the private and public sectors; 127 of these lists had been updated in the previous five years, and 94 were divided into levels of care. There is substantial evidence that the use of national lists of essential drugs has contributed to an improvement in the quality of care and to a considerable saving in drug costs.

1.3 Key components of a national drug policy

A national drug policy is a comprehensive framework in which each component plays an important role in achieving one or more of the general objectives of the policy (access, quality and rational use). The policy should balance the various goals and objectives, creating a complete and consistent entity. For example, access to essential drugs can only be achieved through rational selection, affordable prices, sustainable financing and reliable health and supply systems. Each of the four components of the "access framework" is essential but not sufficient in itself to ensure access. Similarly, rational drug use depends on many factors, such as rational selection, regulatory measures, educational strategies and financial incentives.

Table 1 lists the key components of a national drug policy and shows how they relate to the three main objectives of the policy.

Table 1

Components of a national drug policy, linked to key policy objectives			
Objectives: **Components:**	**Access**	**Quality**	**Rational use**
Selection of essential drugs	X	(X)	X
Affordability	X		
Drug financing	X		
Supply systems	X		(X)
Regulation and quality assurance		X	X
Rational use			X
Research	X	X	X
Human resources	X	X	X
Monitoring and evaluation	X	X	X

X = direct link; (X) = indirect link

As can be seen from the Table, most components cannot be linked to one objective only. The components are briefly summarized below and are discussed in detail in Part II (Chapters 4–12).

Selection of essential drugs

Drug selection, preferably linked to national clinical guidelines, is a crucial step in ensuring access to essential drugs and in promoting rational drug use, because no public sector or health insurance system can afford to supply or reimburse all drugs that are available on the market. Key policy issues are:

- the adoption of the essential drugs concept to identify priorities for government involvement in the pharmaceutical sector, and especially for drug supply in the public sector and for reimbursement schemes;

- procedures to define and update the national list(s) of essential drugs;

- selection mechanisms for traditional and herbal medicines.

Affordability

Affordable prices are an important prerequisite for ensuring access to essential drugs in the public and private sectors. Key policy issues are:

- government commitment to ensuring access through increased affordability;
- for all drugs: reduction of drug taxes, tariffs and distribution margins; pricing policy;
- for multi-source products: promotion of competition through generic policies, generic substitution and good procurement practices;
- for single-source products: price negotiations, competition through price information and therapeutic substitution, and TRIPS-compliant measures such as compulsory licensing, "early workings" of patented drugs for generic manufacturers and parallel imports.

Drug financing

Drug financing is another essential component of policies to improve access to essential drugs. Key policy issues are:

- commitment to measures to improve efficiency and reduce waste;
- increased government funding for priority diseases, and the poor and disadvantaged;
- promotion of drug reimbursement as part of public and private health insurance schemes;
- use and scope of user charges as a (temporary) drug financing option;
- use of and limits of development loans for drug financing;
- guidelines for drug donations.

Supply systems

The fourth essential component of strategies to increase access to essential drugs is a reliable supply system. Key policy issues are:

- public–private mix in drug supply and distribution systems;
- commitment to good pharmaceutical procurement practices in the public sector;
- publication of price information on raw materials and finished products;
- drug supply systems in acute emergencies;
- inventory control, and prevention of theft and waste;
- disposal of unwanted or expired drugs.

Regulation and quality assurance

The drug regulatory authority is the agency that develops and implements most of the legislation and regulations on pharmaceuticals, to ensure the quality, safety and efficacy of drugs, and the accuracy of product information. Key policy issues are:

- government commitment to drug regulation, including the need to ensure a sound legal basis and adequate human and financial resources;

- independence and transparency of the drug regulatory agency; relations between the drug regulatory agency and the ministry of health (MoH);

- stepwise approach to drug evaluation and registration; definition of current and medium-term registration procedures;

- commitment to good manufacturing practices (GMP), inspection and law enforcement;

- access to drug control facilities;

- commitment to regulation of drug promotion;

- regulation of traditional and herbal medicines;

- need and potential for systems of adverse drug reaction monitoring;

- international exchange of information.

Rational use

The rational use of drugs means that patients receive medicines appropriate for their clinical needs, in doses that meet their individual requirements, for an adequate period of time, and at the lowest cost to them and their community. Irrational drug use by prescribers and consumers is a very complex problem, which calls for the implementation of many different interventions at the same time. Efforts to promote rational drug use should also cover the use of traditional and herbal medicines. Key policy issues are:

- development of evidence-based clinical guidelines, as the basis for training, prescribing, drug utilization review, drug supply and drug reimbursement;

- establishment and support of drugs and therapeutics committees;

- promotion of the concepts of essential drugs, rational drug use and generic prescribing in basic and in-service training of health professionals;

- the need and potential for training informal drug sellers;

- continuing education of health care providers and independent, unbiased drug information;

- consumer education, and ways to deliver it;

- financial incentives to promote rational drug use;

- regulatory and managerial strategies to promote rational drug use.

Research

Operational research facilitates the implementation, monitoring and evaluation of different aspects of drug policy. It is an essential tool in assessing the drug policy's impact on national health service systems and delivery, in studying the economics of drug supply, in identifying problems related to prescribing and dispensing, and in understanding the sociocultural aspects of drug use. Key policy issues are:

■ the need for operational research in drug access, quality and rational use;

■ the need and potential for involvement in clinical drug research and development.

Human resources development

Human resources development includes the policies and strategies chosen to ensure that there are enough trained and motivated personnel available to implement the components of the national drug policy. Lack of motivation and appropriate expertise has been a decisive factor in the failure to achieve national drug policy objectives. Key policy issues are:

■ government responsibility for planning and overseeing the development and training of the human resources needed for the pharmaceutical sector;

■ definition of minimum education and training requirements for each category of staff;

■ career planning and team building in government service;

■ the need for external assistance (national and international).

Monitoring and evaluation

Monitoring and evaluation are essential components of a national drug policy, and the necessary provisions need to be included in the policy. Key policy issues are:

■ explicit government commitment to the principles of monitoring and evaluation;

■ monitoring of the pharmaceutical sector through regular indicator-based surveys;

■ independent external evaluation of the impact of the national drug policy on all sectors of the community and the economy.

2 The national drug policy process

2.1 Overview of the national drug policy process

A national drug policy involves a complex process of development, implementation and monitoring. First, the policy development process results in the formulation of the national drug policy. Second, strategies and activities aimed at achieving policy objectives are implemented by the various parties. Finally, the effect of these activities is monitored and the programme adjusted if necessary. Throughout the process careful planning and the involvement of all parties are needed, and the political dynamics have to be considered at all times.

Planning

A drug policy without an implementation plan remains a dead document. Careful planning of the implementation steps and activities necessary to arrive at the expected outcome is important throughout the process.

There are various types of plans. The first is probably the strategic plan to develop the policy itself, which should specify the various steps in the development process, and especially plan for the involvement of as many stakeholders as possible. After the policy has been adopted, an implementation plan, or master plan, is needed, which typically covers a 3–5-year period. This details the various activities for each component of the policy. The implementation plan spells out what needs to be done and who is responsible, estimates the budget and proposes a time frame. If resources are insufficient without external input, a set of priority activities should be identified that can be executed within the existing means. The master plan can be broken down into individual annual work plans for the various departments.

Involving all parties

Throughout the policy process (and not only in the development phase) there should be consultation, dialogue and negotiations with all interested groups and stakeholders. These include other ministries (higher education, trade, industry), doctors, pharmacists and nurses, local and international pharmaceutical industries, drug sellers, academia, nongovernmental organizations (NGOs), professional associations and consumer groups. It is also important to consult with provincial and district medical and administrative personnel, and to make an effort to include traditional and herbal medicine practitioners. Other government agencies (such as the drug regulatory agency), insurance companies and groups paying for health care must be involved. The media can be helpful, and support from international organizations is important. It is recommended that the national drug policy committee meets regularly to review the implementation of the policy with all interested parties in a national drug policy forum.

There is likely to be some disagreement among the various stakeholders. For example, drug manufacturers may feel that their commercial interests are threatened, and doctors may fear the loss of clinical freedom. Any party that benefits from the existing situation will be worried about change. It is a real challenge to create and maintain a process that delivers the broad consensus essential to implementing the policy. In general it can be said that the more the existing pharmaceutical system needs to be improved, the more important it is to involve all interested parties in discussing the necessary reforms.

Political dynamics

Formulating and implementing a national drug policy are highly political processes. This is because such a policy usually seeks to achieve equity of access to basic health care, primarily by making the pharmaceutical sector more efficient, cost-effective and responsive to health needs. Such responsiveness may include redistribution of goods and power, leading to increased competition among the groups affected by reform. Given the diverse interests and the economic importance of the issues involved, opposition to the new policy and attempts to change it during implementation can be expected, as happened in Bangladesh and the Philippines.[4,5]

For this reason it is important to identify political allies, and to maintain their support throughout the process. Strategies to deal with opponents should be developed and ways of working with them must be identified. Decisions and priorities touching on the interests of these stakeholders must be balanced on the basis of estimated gains and losses. Strong political leadership and sustained commitment are vital for the formulation and implementation of a national drug policy.

2.2 Formulating a national drug policy

By the end of 1999, 66 countries had formulated or updated their national drug policy within the previous 10 years. Very often an acute emergency or an important political change created a window of opportunity to start the policy formulation process. In some countries this was a change to a government committed to reform; in other countries it was an economic or political change, such as the sudden devaluation of the CFA (Communauté financière d'Afrique) franc, or the collapse of the Union of Soviet Socialist Republics, which created the need to harmonize and improve certain aspects of the pharmaceutical system. Other factors could be a political drive towards expansion of the local industry or the implementation of global trade agreements.[6]

Step 1: Organize the policy process

The ministry of health is the most appropriate national authority to take the lead role in formulating a national drug policy. The first step is to decide how to organize the development process that will identify the structure of the policy, its major objectives and its priority components.

At this stage it is important to identify all the interested parties that need to be involved, the necessary resources, and how these can be obtained. The need for assistance from WHO, donors or countries with relevant experience should also be assessed. This stage can be carried out within the ministry of health with support from a small committee of selected experts.

Step 2: Identify the main problems

In order to set realistic objectives a thorough analysis and understanding of the main problems in the pharmaceutical sector are needed. There are various ways of carrying out an initial situation analysis.

One successful approach has been to bring together a small team of experts, some of whom should have performed similar analyses in other countries. These experts should come not only from the ministry of health but also from other disciplines and backgrounds. They should be asked to examine the situation systematically, to identify the main problems, to make recommendations about what needs to be done and what can be done, and to identify possible approaches. They should act as impartial advisers. Once they have formulated their recommendations, these can be discussed at one or more multidisciplinary workshops, in order to formulate consolidated advice to the government. Examples of such reports are available from the WHO Department of Essential Drugs and Medicines Policy.

Step 3: Make a detailed situation analysis

A more detailed situation analysis of the pharmaceutical sector and its components may be needed. This should further analyse the source of the problems, in order to identify potential solutions, choose the most appropriate strategies, set priorities, and serve as a baseline for future systems of monitoring and evaluation.

Step 4: Set goals and objectives for a national drug policy

Once the main problems have been defined, goals can be set and priority objectives identified. For instance, if one of the priority problems is lack of access to essential drugs, one of the priority objectives should be to improve the selection, affordability and distribution of essential drugs.

The selection of appropriate strategies to achieve the objective is more complex, since it may involve choosing from among very different approaches. A workshop involving a small number of key policy-makers may be helpful. The situation analysis should justify the choices and serve as the basis for decisions.

Once the main objectives and strategies have been outlined, they should be discussed with all interested parties. Broad consultation and careful consideration of conflicting interests and structural constraints are necessary to set achievable objectives and to formulate appropriate strategies to attain them.

Step 5: Draft the text of the policy

Once a thorough analysis of the situation and an outline of the main goals, objectives and approaches have been completed, a draft text of the national drug policy should be prepared. It should set out the general objectives of the policy. In most countries this will be to ensure that essential drugs are accessible to the entire population; that the drugs are safe, efficacious and of good quality; and that they are used rationally by health professionals and consumers. The specific objectives should also be described, followed in each case by the strategy to be adopted. Drafting of the policy can be done by a small group of experts who have been involved in the earlier stages of the process. Examples of national drug policy documents from other countries may be consulted.

Step 6: Circulate and revise the draft policy

The draft document should be widely circulated for comments, first within the ministry of health, then in other government ministries and departments, and finally to relevant institutions and organizations outside the government, including the private and academic sectors. Endorsement by government sectors responsible for planning, finance and education is important since the successful implementation of many elements of the policy will depend on their support as well. Once this wide consultation is complete, the draft document should be revised in the light of the comments received, and finalized.

Step 7: Secure formal endorsement of the policy

In some countries the document can then go to the cabinet or parliament for endorsement. In others it will remain an administrative document that serves as a basis for implementation plans and changes in the law and regulations. In some countries the entire national drug policy document has become law. This is a powerful demonstration of political commitment but it can also cause problems, as future adjustments to the policy may become difficult. It is therefore recommended that only certain enabling components of the policy are incorporated into law, without too many operational details.

Step 8: Launch the national drug policy

Introducing a national drug policy is much more than a technical task. To a large extent the policy's success will depend on the level of understanding of different sectors of society, and on their support for its objectives. The implications and benefits for all interested parties should therefore be stressed.

The policy should be promoted through a clear and well-designed information campaign. Public endorsement by respected experts and opinion leaders can be very useful. Information should be disseminated through a variety of channels to reach different target groups. The media can play a major role in ensuring public understanding and support for the policy. Some countries have organized high profile launches.

2.3 Implementing a national drug policy

A policy, however carefully formulated, is worthless if it is not implemented. Every drug policy needs an overall implementation plan or "master plan"; each component of the policy needs a detailed strategy and specific action plans. In this section some general observations on implementation are made. More detailed technical recommendations for each component of a national drug policy are made in subsequent chapters (see also Box 1).

Priorities for implementation

For each country the priorities for implementation will be different. For example, when health care coverage is broad and access to drugs is not a problem, rational use and the cost of drugs are likely to be of concern. In such a situation, implementation of a drug policy will focus on regulating the market and on containing costs without decreasing sustainable access and equity. In least developed countries total spending on health and pharmaceuticals may be very low, and the private sector not geared to meeting the needs of the majority of the population. In this situation the focus of the policy will be more on increasing access to essential drugs.

Priorities for implementation should be based on the severity of the problems, and on the potential for success in achieving the objective and making an impact with available resources.

Master plan and work plans

The national drug policy leads to an implementation plan or master plan, which may cover a 3–5-year period. This implementation plan spells out for each component of the policy what needs to be done and who is responsible, estimates the budget requirement and proposes a rough time frame. If resources are insufficient without external input, a set of priority activities should be identified that can be executed within existing means. Potential donor inputs should also be included, and gaps in funding can be identified as a guide for future donor support. The master plan facilitates monitoring and follow-up, and it is important that it is communicated to all parties involved.

The master plan should be broken down into annual action plans and work plans, which should be carefully developed with the various agencies involved in implementation. These plans should outline the approaches and activities for each component, specifying in detail who is responsible, listing the major tasks, and describing the target output, the detailed time frame and the exact budget.

Responsibilities in implementation

As lead agency, the ministry of health should oversee and coordinate all activities, and monitor the extent of implementation and the achievement of targets. In some countries a separate unit within the ministry, with its own budget and personnel, acts as the coordinating body.

Apart from the coordinating body, it is recommended that a national consultative forum is created to oversee policy implementation. This is essential to create and maintain countrywide support for the policy, and to ensure that the major stakeholders remain informed and involved. The same could be done for some specific policy components, for example, all activities dealing with quality assurance or rational drug use.

National institutions, such as the drug regulatory agency, the pharmacy department in the ministry of health, the central medical stores, and district or provincial health offices, are key players in drug policy implementation. So too are other agencies dealing with finance, trade, economic planning and education. Given the multisectoral nature of pharmaceutical issues it is important not only to *obtain* but also to *maintain* consensus on the policy objectives. This can be achieved by agreement on implementation plans and through regular progress reports.

Financial resources

It is important to match the strategies and action plans with available financial resources. Allocations from government funds and revenue from drug registrations and fees are the usual funding sources. The responsible agencies should have a mechanism for actively seeking funds and be able to secure regular funding from the government. Contributions from international and local donors are also possible sources. However, there should be no conflict of interest in accepting donor contributions, for example, when donors are interested in funding activities that are of low priority in the national drug policy.

Box 1

Practical aspects of policy implementation

A drug policy can be successfully implemented only if the government is committed and proactive. Some successful strategies are:

- At an early stage, prepare the relevant legislative structure to enable the development and implementation of the national drug policy.
- Seize a window of political opportunity, such as a specific political change or developments in neighbouring countries, to advance policy development or implementation.
- Start implementing the policy in relatively easy subject areas, in order to ensure initial high visibility and success, and support for the policy at the critical early stage.
- Adopt a flexible approach; be prepared to postpone an activity if more time is needed to prepare for it, to explain it and to build consensus for it.
- Have national experts and respected political figures publicly express support for the policy and vouch for its technical soundness. It is important that the public feels confident about the policy.
- Mobilize key groups in society to support the policy. Consumer organizations, trade unions, religious organizations and the media, for example, can be important in building such support.
- Anticipate shifts in opponents' positions, and identify strategies to involve them and to win their support. For example, the pharmaceutical industry may oppose drug pricing policies and the introduction of an essential drugs list, but will usually support strategies to strengthen drug regulation and improve drug quality assurance.
- Create constituencies that support the policy both inside and outside the government. This is crucial to the policy's long-term success and sustainability.

Regional cooperation

Regional cooperation can be useful in implementing drug policies. Countries, institutions and organizations can share information, expertise, skills and facilities. Exchanging experiences helps to ensure that best practices are promoted, that mistakes are not repeated and that limited resources are used effectively.

Increasingly, countries cooperate on a regional basis on a wide variety of economic and policy issues. The Association of South-East Asian Nations (ASEAN), the European Union (EU) and the Organization of African Unity (OAU) are just three examples of regional partnerships.

Box 2

ASEAN cooperation in pharmaceuticals

For more than a decade, the ASEAN countries have collaborated in various aspects of the pharmaceutical sector. The following factors have contributed to success:
- Similarity in language and cultural affinity of most of the cooperating countries.
- Consultative and participatory planning by all countries from an early stage.
- Technical, financial and organizational support from international organizations such as WHO and the United Nations Development Programme.
- Careful selection of priority areas for cooperation with an immediate and visible impact.
- Continuing and sustained activities over a period of time, with one lead country coordinating each project and other countries actively participating.
- Dissemination of outputs and relevant information from each project to all participating countries at annual meetings.
- A political climate in the region conducive to cooperation in many areas.
- Absence of significant opposition from any sector or vested interest in any of the participating countries.

Sharing information and technical expertise can be particularly effective if the policies and strategies are mutually relevant and easy to adapt. Harmonization of drug regulatory standards can be one outcome of successful technical and regulatory cooperation among countries. Harmonization in these areas could lead to a more economical use of human, animal and material resources, and to the development of regionally or internationally agreed standards. However, the issue of sovereignty has to be considered. During the process of harmonization each country must ensure that the areas being harmonized can be implemented and are relevant to national interests.

Technical cooperation with WHO

WHO can provide a forum for exchange of information, and can promote cooperation through regional and international training courses and through inter-country research projects. WHO collaborating centres and other centres of excellence are also involved in training and research, forming professional networks and exchanging information among cooperating countries.

New information technologies present a wealth of opportunities for efficient and low-cost exchange of information, consultation, collaboration and technical cooperation. WHO's Medicines web site contains most of the technical information and key documents relevant for developing national drug policies.[7] Another key reference is *Managing drug supply,* a textbook developed by Management Sciences for Health (MSH) in close collaboration with WHO.[8]

A training course on drug policy issues is conducted regularly for key officials involved in pharmaceuticals,[a] and the International Conference of Drug Regulatory Authorities (ICDRA) meets every two years to discuss drug regulatory matters.

---

[a] Detailed information on these and other courses and conferences is available from the WHO Department of Essential Drugs and Medicine Policy, Geneva; or from national WHO offices.

2.4 Monitoring and evaluation

Why are monitoring and evaluation important?

Monitoring and evaluating the impact of a national drug policy are challenging. Apart from a lack of time, human resources and budget, there is often a basic lack of understanding of the value of monitoring in the first place, and even a certain resistance to objectively or critically reviewing the effects of activities formulated in the master plan.

Monitoring is a form of continuous review which gives a picture of the implementation of planned activities and indicates whether targets are being met. It can be carried out using a combination of various methods, including supervisory visits and both routine and sentinel reporting.

Evaluation is a way of analysing progress towards meeting agreed objectives and goals. It should build on, and use, monitoring systems. At the start of a programme it is used to provide a clear needs assessment. A mid-term evaluation can provide valuable information about whether the programme is working, and if not, why not. Final evaluation allows a complete review of programme achievements from which lessons can be drawn for the future.

A system for monitoring and evaluation is a constructive management tool that enables a continuous assessment of progress, and helps to make the necessary management decisions. It also provides transparency and accountability, and creates a standard by which comparisons can be made between countries and areas and over time. All of this may produce the necessary evidence that progress is being made (or not), in order to support the policy in discussions with interested parties and policy-makers. Some practical aspects are presented in Box 1.

Indicators for monitoring national drug policies

To determine whether adequate progress is being achieved it is helpful to set realistic targets or performance standards. Indicators can be selected and used to measure changes, make comparisons and assess whether the targets are being met. If indicators are used they should be clear, useful, measurable, reliable and valid.

WHO and MSH have done a great deal of operational research to develop and refine indicators for monitoring drug policies.[9,10] Currently there are four categories of drug policy indicators: background information, structural indicators, process indicators and outcome indicators. It is possible to use selected subsets of these indicators to meet the needs of countries.

WHO and MSH have also agreed on a subset of core indicators for routine use and sentinel reporting. These indicators are highly standardized so that trends can be identified. A detailed manual on their use is available.[11] Data collection is relatively easy, so that monitoring can be done on a regular basis. Core indicators cover the following aspects:

- access to essential drugs, and other indicators on drug financing schemes, and public supply management; these provide information on access to essential drugs;

- functions and efficiency of the drug regulatory authority, the quality control laboratory and how drugs are handled to maintain good quality; these provide information about drug quality;

- drug prescribing and dispensing, use of the list of essential drugs and clinical guidelines; these provide information about drug use patterns.

Routine reporting or sentinel reporting?

A routine reporting system, as part of a drug management information system, can provide much of the information needed to monitor the drug policy's implementation. However, in reality much of the routine information is not collected systematically and whatever is collected is rarely used. With a sentinel reporting system a selected sample of health facilities is regularly surveyed. Some countries, such as Zimbabwe, have successfully used a sentinel reporting system to collect, every two years, standard information about the status, strengths and weaknesses of the national pharmaceutical system. This has proved to be a very useful management tool.[12]

Who can use the results?

The indicator-based method of assessing the pharmaceutical situation can be useful for various parties involved in the pharmaceutical field. Policy-makers, implementers and managers can get a clear picture of the problems in the country so that they can reassess their strategies and priorities. Results can be used as a guide to setting priorities and to strengthening those strategies that can have the best impact.

Results can also be used by the government and health ministry to synchronize policies. For example, a low level of availability and affordability of essential drugs could indicate that the directions on health and drug financing should be reviewed. Economic policies may be too focused on joining the global economy without looking into the implications for drug pricing, or affordability and availability of relevant drugs. The presence of substandard drug products in the market could indicate the need to assess the implications of the government's emphasis on a free market that allows more products and business entities than the drug regulatory authority (DRA) can efficiently regulate.

International agencies and donors can use the results to focus on priority areas that need support and to determine the viability of investing resources in areas where best impact can be achieved. Professional groups and NGOs can also be guided on areas where advocacy campaigns and information can be focused.

Multi-country comparative evaluations

Multi-country studies based on standard methodologies can assist national policy-makers in learning about innovative approaches that may be applicable in their own country. They also encourage international exchanges and collaboration on drug policy issues. One example is the 12-country study on national drug policy monitoring.[13] Its results indicate that in most countries the structure and the system are in place, but that it is much easier to create structures than to make them work. One example is the DRA: although it has the mandate to register drugs and inspect manufacturer and retail outlets, enforcement of regulations is often limited. In many countries public drug financing is weak.

The core indicators mentioned above are collected by WHO for international comparisons and are kept in the Organization's database and used for WHO's report on the world drug situation.[14]

Box 3

Practical aspects of monitoring national drug policies

- Identify the right questions: focus on questions with answers that are relevant for management decisions.
- Limit data collection to data that are relevant and are likely to be used. If too many data are collected the process will become expensive, and data analysis will become too complicated and probably less accurate.
- Establish a reliable data collection system; remember that the data will be reliable only if they are also of relevance to the people who collect them. Wherever possible, build on and strengthen existing systems; data collection should as much as possible be built into the routine functioning of the system. This requires staff to be trained and resources to be allocated. Rapid feed-back of results is important.
- Apart from being used by district or provincial health managers, the aggregated results should flow back to the central policy and management level, and be used for management decisions at the central level. If the data are used to prepare a monitoring report, the report should be shared with all those who contributed to it, including those who collected the data.

Periodic evaluations of the national drug policy

The national drug policy should be periodically evaluated, for example every four years. Independent consultants or professionals from other countries or from WHO may be invited to complement a national evaluation team. Such evaluations should form an integral part of the pharmaceutical master plan, with the necessary resources allocated from the start.

3 Legislation

3.1 Importance of legislation and regulations

A legislative framework is needed in order to implement and enforce the various components of a national drug policy, and to regulate the activities of the different parties in both the public and private sectors. Permitting the circulation of poor-quality, ineffective products and harmful ingredients in a country has an impact on the population's health and on the national economy. Lack of legislation and regulations on other aspects of pharmaceuticals, such as financing, supply and the use of drugs, affects cost-effectiveness in health delivery.

Two types of legal framework cover pharmaceuticals. Laws are passed by a country's legislative bodies, and are formulated in general terms to meet current and future needs. Regulations enable government authorities to set out in more detail how the laws should be interpreted, and how they will be implemented and enforced. Regulations can be changed more easily than laws, and create the necessary flexibility in a changing environment. In some countries, regulations require only the approval of the head of a ministry or department.

Legislation and regulations ensure that the responsibilities, qualifications, rights and roles of each party are defined and recognized (including those of medical practitioners, pharmacists and the drug regulatory authority). They also create the legal basis enabling the regulatory control of activities such as drug manufacture, import, export, marketing, prescribing, dispensing and distribution, and the enforcement of such laws and regulations.

The purpose of the legislation is therefore the same as that of the drug policy: to ensure that only safe, effective, quality drugs are produced, imported and distributed, and that these drugs are made available, as well as managed and used appropriately.

3.2 Framework for drug legislation

What is covered by the legislation?

Pharmaceutical legislation is mostly concerned with ensuring that effective and safe drugs of good quality are made available, and that correct information is provided about them. These tasks are covered in drug laws, pharmacy acts and drug regulations. The drug regulatory authority is the enforcing body.

There are also other laws and regulations that may support the implementation of the national drug policy, such as those that support generic substitution, those relating to patents and intellectual property rights, and tax laws. In some countries there are laws and regulations that deal with prescribing and dispensing practices to ensure the appropriate use of drugs. The most important aspects of a national drug policy which need legislative and regulatory support are listed in Table 2.

Table 2

Examples of components of a national drug policy which need political and legislative support

Component	Political and legislative[b] support on:
Selection of essential drugs	• Use of the national list of essential drugs • Selection and use of traditional medicines
Affordability	• Removal of import taxes on essential drugs • Distribution margins • Pricing policy • Generic policy, generic substitution • Equity pricing • Parallel import[c] • Compulsory licensing[c]
Drug financing	• Increased government funding of drugs for priority diseases, the poor and disadvantaged • User charges, cost-sharing mechanisms • Support for health insurance and social security • Drug donations
Supply systems	• Public drug supply based on essential drugs list • Public-private mix in drug supply and distribution • Support to national pharmaceutical industry • Disposal of unwanted or expired drugs
Regulation and quality assurance	• Establishment and funding of the drug regulatory agency • Good manufacturing practices and other quality standards • Licensing of products, premises and personnel • Inspection • Quality control • Regulation of traditional and herbal medicines
Rational use	• Scheduling of drugs (over-the-counter, prescription-only) • Minimum requirements of professional training • Essential drugs concept as basis for training curricula • Training of informal drug sellers • Use of financial incentives for prescribers • Dissociation of prescribing/dispensing functions • Drug promotion
Research	• Clinical trials

[b] Legislative support includes laws, decrees and regulations.
[c] In accordance with the TRIPS Agreement

Legislation framework

Legislative models and structures for drug regulation vary from country to country, but the basic elements listed below represent a reasonable common framework. The applicable legislation must be broad in its scope in order to address all the essential issues and be flexible enough to make the legislation specific to problems. The list below can be useful as the basis for planning new drug laws or for revising existing legislation.

Box 4

Elements of drug legislation

What should be regulated
- Premises, persons and practices involved in the manufacture, importation, distribution, procurement, supply and sale of drugs, as well as the promotion and advertising of drugs.
- Drug products.

Who regulates
- Governments have primary responsibility, but public and private professional associations also have a role to play.

Scope/extent of regulation
- Geographical area.

Which sanctions
- Administrative measures.
- Legal sanctions (warnings, fines, withdrawal of licences, imprisonment).

Organization of the text and general provisions
- Title or name of the law.
- Date of entry into operation of the entire law or certain parts, sections and articles.
- Area of operation (geographical) and application (state, private and public sector).
- Purposes and objective.
- Relationship to other existing laws.
- Definitions of selected terms and concepts, exclusions.
- Statutory powers, duties and responsibilities of the regulatory authority, its organization, resources and staff.
- Licensing and registration system (products, companies and individuals in the contexts of manufacture, import, export, transit, procurement, distribution, prescribing, dispensing, storage, use); statutory requirements, standards and procedures.
- Information (labelling), advertising and promotion.
- Enforcement procedures (seizures), penal provisions and administrative penalties.
- Special issues (patents, pricing, clinical trials, post-marketing surveillance, national essential drugs list and formulary, generic drugs, traditional medicines, orphan drugs).
- Regulation-making scope and power.

3.3 Developing drug legislation and regulations

In some countries there are opportunities to review all relevant drug laws and bring them together in one law, while in other countries drug issues are covered in different laws and regulations.

In drafting or revising drug legislation it is important, first, to make a full inventory of existing laws and regulations, and carefully decide what type of legislation is required. Then, legal experts should collaborate closely with health experts and other stakeholders in drafting the new text. After drafting, a wide consultative process is needed to inform interested parties and to enable them to comment and express their concerns. At this time it is important to ensure that there is political support for the proposed changes and that this support is maintained throughout the process.

When writing the law, the practicalities of future enforcement should be kept in mind. If there are no strategies, facilities and resources for implementation and enforcement, legislation on its own will achieve nothing. A law with modest aims and objectives that is properly enforced is preferable to a more comprehensive one that cannot be implemented.

Box 5

Some practical aspects of developing or updating drug legislation

- Pharmaceutical legislation and regulations cannot be developed or updated in a vacuum, but must fit into the country's existing legal framework. It is imperative to define clearly the objectives of drug legislation in relation to national health objectives, government policies and available resources.
- The legislation should cover the basic principles. It should also enable the issuing of lower-level legal acts and regulations covering technical and operational details, which can be changed more easily.
- Political commitment is required and all stakeholders must be consulted. Moreover, opposition may be mounted by those whose interests will be affected. This can often result in lengthy negotiations, and drafting and passing laws and regulations can therefore be time-consuming.

PART TWO

Key components of a national drug policy

4 Selection of essential drugs

Key policy issues

Drug selection, preferably linked to national clinical guidelines, is a crucial step in ensuring access to essential drugs and in promoting rational drug use, because no public sector or health insurance system can afford to supply or reimburse all drugs that are available on the market. Key policy issues are:
- the adoption of the essential drugs concept to identify priorities for government involvement in the pharmaceutical sector, and especially for drug supply in the public sector and for reimbursement schemes;
- procedures to define and update the national list(s) of essential drugs;
- selection mechanisms for traditional and herbal medicines.

4.1 Essential drugs

The selection of essential drugs is one of the core principles of a national drug policy because it helps to set priorities for all aspects of the pharmaceutical system.

WHO has defined essential drugs as "those that satisfy the needs of the majority of the population and therefore should be available at all times, in adequate amounts in appropriate dosage forms and at a price the individual and the community can afford".[15] This is a global concept that can be applied in any country, in the private and public sectors and at different levels of the health care system.

Essential drugs concept

The concept of essential drugs is that a limited number of carefully selected drugs based on agreed clinical guidelines leads to more rational prescribing, to a better supply of drugs and to lower costs. The reasons are obvious:

- Essential drugs which are selected on the basis of safe and cost-effective clinical guidelines lead to more rational prescribing,[16] and therefore to higher quality of care and better value for money;

- Training of health workers and drug information in general can be more focused;

- Prescribers gain more experience with fewer drugs, and recognize drug interactions and adverse reactions more easily;

- Quality assurance, procurement, storage, distribution and dispensing are all easier with a reduced number of drugs;

- The procurement of fewer items in larger quantities results in more price competition and economies of scale.

All of this is even more important in resource-poor situations where the availability of drugs in the public sector is often erratic. Under such circumstances measures to ensure a regular supply of essential drugs will result in real health gains and in increased confidence in health services.

Practical implications of the essential drugs concept

National essential drugs lists and national drug formularies, together with clinical guidelines, should serve as the basis of formal education and in-service training of health professionals, and of public education about drug use. They should also serve as the main basis for public sector drug procurement and distribution, as well as for drug donations.

Insurance schemes often use a limited list of drugs, the costs of which they will reimburse. This is one of the most common applications of the principle of selection in developed countries. In developing countries health insurance is less widespread, but coverage is growing and schemes are generally based on reimbursement for essential drugs. In view of the rapidly rising cost of drugs in most countries it can safely be stated that any health insurance scheme would need a process of drug selection one way or another.

Essential drugs lists and teaching about the benefits of drug selection could also be used to influence practice in the private sector, for example through the basic training of medical students, and programmes of continuing medical education with universities and professional associations.

4.2 Old problems and new challenges

By the end of 1999, 156 Member States had an official national essential drugs list, and 127 of the lists had been updated in the previous five years. Most of these lists are linked to national clinical guidelines used for training and supervision. They also serve as a guide for drug supply in the public sector, drug benefits within reimbursement schemes, drug donations and local production. The concept of using fewer drugs more effectively therefore seems to be widespread, yet it is not always simple to implement fully, and various old and new challenges need to be considered.

Gaining further acceptance of the principle

There may be opposition to the use of the essential drugs list. Prescribers may see it as undermining their clinical freedom, while pharmacists may be worried about the financial implications. Manufacturers may fear that their market will be eroded, and consumers may think that they are being offered second-rate cheap drugs. If these concerns are not addressed, the concept of selection and the use of an essential drugs list will not be accepted. This is why the selection process should be consultative, and why informing and educating those affected is important.

Promoting essential drugs in the private sector

There has been considerable experience with the use of an essential drugs list in the public sector. However, in most low- and middle-income countries the majority of people are treated with drugs from the private sector, paid for out-of-pocket. Too often these consumers are prescribed or dispensed high-priced drugs, often in small quantities, rather than therapeutic amounts of essential drugs. Promotion of non-essential drugs often results in over-treatment of mild illnesses, inadequate treatment of serious illnesses, and overuse of antibiotics. Widespread prescription and sale of non-essential drugs means that households, especially poor households, are not getting the best health care value for their money and may ultimately not receive the treatment they need.

Promoting the essential drugs concept in the private sector continues to present countries with a considerable challenge. Private health insurance programmes and enlightened professional associations are often the best entry point for introducing cost-effective drug selection into the private sector.

Donations of non-essential drugs

The donation of non-essential drugs can undermine the acceptance and implementation of the selection process and adherence to evidence-based clinical guidelines. WHO, together with many other organizations, has developed interagency guidelines to address this issue.[17] The key point in this respect is that drug donations should be limited to drugs on the national essential drugs list, unless specifically requested and agreed upon otherwise.

4.3 Strategies for the selection of essential drugs

Two-step process

The selection of essential drugs is a two-step process. Market approval of a pharmaceutical product is usually granted on the basis of efficacy, safety and quality, and rarely on the basis of a comparison with other products already on the market or of cost. The regulatory decision defines the availability of a drug in the market. In addition to this, most public drug procurement and insurance schemes have mechanisms to limit procurement or reimbursements of drug costs. For these decisions an evaluation process is necessary, based on a comparison between various drug products and on considerations of value for money. This second step leads to a list of essential drugs.

A list of essential drugs is best developed for different levels of care, and on the basis of clinical guidelines for common diseases and complaints that can and should be diagnosed and treated at that level. A good balance of expert opinions and evidence of effectiveness and cost-effectiveness should lead the development of clinical guidelines. Both these guidelines and the essential drugs lists for the different levels of care must be updated regularly, preferably every two years.

WHO Model List of Essential Drugs

The Model List of Essential Drugs is intended as a model for the second step in the selection process. It has been updated by the WHO Expert Committee on the Use of Essential Drugs every two years since 1977. The Model List of 1999 contains 306 active ingredients and is divided into a main list and a complementary list.[15] Drugs are specified by international nonproprietary name (INN) or generic name without reference to brand names or specific manufacturers.[18]

Selection criteria

The treatment recommended and the drugs selected depend on many factors, such as the pattern of prevalent diseases, treatment facilities, the training and experience of available personnel, financial resources, and genetic, demographic and environmental factors. The following criteria are used by the WHO Expert Committee on the Use of Essential Drugs:

- only drugs for which sound and adequate evidence of efficacy and safety in a variety of settings is available should be selected;

- relative cost-effectiveness is a major consideration in the choice of drugs. In comparisons between drugs, the total cost of the treatment – not only the unit cost of the drug – must be considered, and be compared with its efficacy;

- in some cases, the choice may also be influenced by other factors such as pharmaco-kinetic properties or by local considerations such as the availability of facilities for manufacture or storage;

- each drug selected must be available in a form in which adequate quality, including bioavailability, can be ensured; its stability under the expected conditions of storage and use must be determined;

- most essential drugs should be formulated as single compounds. Fixed-ratio combination products are acceptable only when the dosage of each ingredient meets the requirements of a defined population group, and when the combination has a proven advantage over single compounds administered separately, in terms of therapeutic effect, safety or patient adherence to treatment.

Selection process

The process by which drugs are selected is critical. An essential drugs list that is imposed from above will not reflect the needs of the users or be accepted by them. It is therefore very important that: the process is consultative and transparent; the selection criteria are explicit; selection of the drugs is linked to evidence-based clinical guidelines; and the clinical guidelines and the list are divided into levels of care, and that both are regularly reviewed and updated. Clinical guidelines and the list should be reviewed at least every two years, and their use and the impact should be monitored.

A standing committee should be appointed to give technical advice. This committee should include people from different fields, such as medicine, nursing, clinical pharmacology, pharmacy, public health, consumer affairs as well as health workers at grass-roots level. Formal and informal consultations should be organized with interested parties, including representatives of professional bodies, pharmaceutical manufacturers, consumer organizations and the government budget and finance group. However, the final drug selection by the committee members should be carried out independently.

An important principle that needs to be accepted by the committee is that not all evidence is equally strong. For example, the result of a meta-analysis of several clinical trials carries more weight than the result of an observational study without controls, and much more than the personal experiences of individual experts. The strength of the evidence defines the strength of the recommendation.

When the clinical guidelines and the essential drugs list are finalized and printed, they should be launched and made widely available. In case of an update, it may be useful to issue an information leaflet that summarizes the changes or to make the changes known through a newsletter or drug bulletin.

4.4 Traditional and herbal medicines

In many countries, traditional medicine continues to be widely practised and its place in health care should be considered in the broader development of health policy. When developing a national drug policy, countries may wish to include traditional and herbal medicines within its scope. When introducing traditional and herbal medicines into organized health care, countries should:

- identify the health conditions that can be treated with traditional and herbal medicines;

- develop an appropriate methodology and technology for the identification, development and production of traditional and herbal medicines;[19–22]

- undertake studies to evaluate the quality and safety of traditional and herbal medicines, and evidence of their efficacy;[23]

- encourage patients, physicians, pharmacists and other health workers to be alert to adverse reactions and to notify them where possible.

Traditional and herbal medicines are usually known by local names, which often vary from country to country. There are several national and regional pharmacopoeias that include monographs on medicinal plant materials and herbal medicines. However, there is no well-recognized convention regarding nomenclature, except official names for medicinal plant materials based on the legitimate Latin binominal name of the plant of origin (genus, species, authority and family). A series of WHO monographs on selected medicinal plants provide some information on this.[24]

A committee including traditional health practitioners and healers, and experts in pharmacognosy, toxicology and related fields should establish the criteria for selection of traditional and herbal medicines for health care systems. Use of the WHO guidelines for the assessment of herbal medicines is recommended.[23] The drug regulatory authority should consider developing regulatory measures on traditional and herbal medicines.[25]

5 Affordability

5.1 Challenges

New essential drugs are often expensive

Affordable prices are important for both public and private sectors. The issue of affordability is becoming more important because resistance to well-known antibiotics, which are widely available as generic products, is increasing. New essential drugs for the treatment of some infectious diseases, such as malaria, tuberculosis and HIV/AIDS, are often very costly.

Market failure

In a perfect market, buyers and consumers are left to transact their business, and the balance between supply and demand results in a reasonable price. However, conditions for such markets are rarely met in pharmaceuticals because of the following factors:[26]

■ *Information imbalance.* The patient knows less than the prescriber or the dispenser about the efficacy, quality and appropriateness of the drug. This can result in misleading advice and miscommunication, and ultimately inappropriate drug use. For markets to work properly both buyers and sellers should have complete information.

■ *Failure of competition.* This occurs when market power is created through exclusive rights, such as patents and trademarks, and when production is concentrated in a small number of suppliers.

■ *Externalities.* Some health services (such as childhood immunizations, and treatment of tuberculosis and sexually transmitted diseases) benefit not only the person using them but others whose risk of illness is reduced. These third party or "spillover" benefits are externalities. Such health services, with large public health benefits for society as a whole, cannot be left to the market and justify public investment.

International trade agreements

The Uruguay Round of trade negotiations under the General Agreement on Tariffs and Trade was concluded in 1994. The World Trade Organization (WTO) was created to administer the new multilateral trade agreements that include the comprehensive TRIPS Agreement (Trade-Related Aspects of Intellectual Property Rights). TRIPS sets minimum standards in the field of intellectual property and obliges WTO Member States to grant full patent protection (both process and product patents) for at least 20 years; this includes pharmaceuticals.

Social benefits may arise from patent protection, through the development of new drugs. Developing countries should be aware of the implications for local pharmaceutical production and the possible increased cost of some finished products in the future. The impact of the TRIPS Agreement on access to drugs should be carefully monitored and evaluated.[27,28]

Industry consolidation

The pharmaceutical industry is changing as the result of a wave of mergers, acquisitions and strategic alliances. The generic industry is also consolidating.

5.2 Strategies to increase affordability

For all drugs: reducing taxes, tariffs and margins, pricing policy

Price controls may be considered if the market is not functioning well. The first approach is to reduce or abolish any import duties on essential drugs. Secondly, pricing policies could be considered, based on: actual costs (i.e. on manufacturing or importation costs plus a fixed mark-up for the wholesaler and retailer); control of profit margins; comparison with prices in other countries or with other drugs in the same therapeutic category (benchmark or reference pricing); or direct price negotiation with manufacturers of patented or other single-source medicines without therapeutic substitutes. More information is available elsewhere.[26]

For multi-source products: promote competition

Multi-source products could be generic drugs or therapeutic equivalents. The important economic characteristic of generic drugs is that their name identifies the product rather than the supplier. Using generic names promotes price competition among equal medicines from different sources or suppliers, identified by international nonproprietary names (INN). Generic drugs are substantially less expensive than branded products. The use of generics is often promoted in the public and private sectors to reduce drug costs, and increase drug availability and consumer access.

Generic policies, including generic substitution

The use of generic drugs can be promoted at various levels, from procurement to the point of purchase. Competitive bulk procurement by generic name is a central feature of most essential drugs programmes. In the private market, price competition can be encouraged through generic prescribing and generic substitution.

There are four main factors that influence the use of generic drugs and the success of generic drug programmes: supportive legislation, quality assurance capacity, acceptance by prescribers and the public, and economic incentives.

Supportive legislation and regulations indicate that registration of generic drugs is promoted, or at least not obstructed, with a focus on product quality as the safety and efficacy of the active ingredient have already been documented.[29] Tendering and inventory control should be done under generic name, generic prescribing should be promoted, generic substitution should be allowed or, preferably, encouraged. Market entry of generic products can be encouraged by legal provisions for the formulation and registration of generic products before the patent of the original product expires, enabling generic competition immediately after the patent expires. In the private market, drug packages should give the generic name immediately below the brand name, with a specified minimum size of the characters (30–50% of the brand name size in many countries; in some the characters should be of equal size).

With regard to *quality* it is important that the prescribers and the public have full confidence in the quality of generic products. A quality assurance programme should therefore be established with registration, licensing and inspection, and testing of bioavailability and bioequivalence when needed. A list of products for substitution should be published. Legal provisions may allow for the formulation and registration of generic products before the patent of the original product expires, enabling generic competition immediately after the patent expires.

Public and professional acceptance can be achieved through information campaigns, through the obligatory use of generic names in the training of health professionals and for prescribing in public and teaching hospitals. Other possibilities are the use of generic names in formularies, clinical guidelines and drug information bulletins, and a cross-reference list of brand and generic names for all prescribers.

Economic incentives include comparative drug price information, reimbursement in insurance schemes of low-cost generic equivalents, favourable retail fees or margins for generic drugs, and tax incentives for the generic industry.

In all cases a phased introduction is probably the most feasible. Most countries would go through four stages: generic substitution not allowed; generic substitution allowed; generic substitution encouraged; generic substitution obligatory. It is not advisable to jump from the first phase into a system of obligatory generic prescribing – countries which have tried that have all failed. In most countries the market share of generic drugs increases by only a few percent per year.

Good procurement practices

Good procurement practice is relevant for all drug supply systems. However, within the scope of a national drug policy it is especially relevant for the public sector. WHO, the United Nations Children's Fund (UNICEF), the United Nations Population Fund (UNFPA) and the World Bank have defined 12 operational principles for good pharmaceutical procurement.[30] This subject is discussed as part of health systems in Section 7.2, which also covers market intelligence, price information, price negotiations and pooled procurement, all of which help to reduce prices.

For single-source products: equity pricing and competition

The two main approaches to increasing affordability of single-source, mostly patented drugs are equity pricing and increased competition.

Differential or equity pricing

Differential or equity pricing means that the same drug sells at a lower price in poorer countries than in richer country markets. The idea behind the concept is that the poor of the world should not pay for research and development costs, promotional activities and shareholder profits. There are several ways of achieving this, for example lower prices offered by individual manufacturers, incentives to manufacturers through bulk purchasing, and voluntary or compulsory licensing arrangements. Necessary accompaniments to equity pricing are measures to prevent re-export to high-income markets, such as purchase agreements, regulatory measures or separate marketing of the same drug under different brand names in developed and developing countries.

Price information and therapeutic substitution

Competition can be promoted by wide publication of price information,[31] and by allowing substitution and price competition within groups of single-source drugs that are considered therapeutically equivalent. This is called therapeutic substitution. If this mechanism is used it is recommended that lists of drugs that are considered to be therapeutically equivalent, and that can be substituted, are published to guide health workers and consumers.

Promote competition, use of TRIPS-compatible safeguards

National legislation should be enacted which can draw advantage from more open trade and a better-regulated international system. Patents for pharmaceuticals should be managed in an impartial way, safeguarding basic public health principles as well as protecting the interests of the patent holder, as exemplified in the TRIPS Agreement. In adapting their patent legislation to the requirements of the TRIPS Agreement, it is recommended that governments incorporate the safeguards that have been built into the TRIPS Agreement to protect the rights of the public. These safeguards include compulsory licensing and the so-called "early workings" of patented drugs for generic manufacturers. The possibility for parallel import should also be included in national legislation. More information on this issue is available.[27,32,33]

6

Drug financing

Key policy issues

Drug financing is another essential component of policies to improve access to essential drugs. Key policy issues are:

- commitment to measures to improve efficiency and reduce waste;
- increased government funding for priority diseases, and for the poor and disadvantaged;
- promotion of drug reimbursements as part of public and private health insurance schemes;
- use and scope of user charges as a (temporary) drug financing option;
- use of and limits of development loans for drug financing;
- guidelines for drug donations.

Countries vary greatly with respect to income levels, population, health care expenditure and other relevant factors. National spending on pharmaceuticals may vary from US$ 2 to US$ 400 per capita per year. Questions related to drug financing have become increasingly crucial in the formulation and implementation of national drug policies.[34]

6.1 Challenges

Inadequate resources

Ensuring stable and adequate financing for health care is becoming increasingly difficult as a result of the combined effects of economic pressures, continued population growth and the growing burden of disease. Health care resources are stretched by the demographic shift to older populations, with more costly chronic diseases, the emergence of new diseases such as AIDS, and the resurgence of older diseases, such as tuberculosis and malaria, which need increasingly costly drugs because of growing resistance to the earlier drugs.

Achieving equity

Market-oriented "Laissez-faire" policies are not geared to protecting the needs of the poorest people, and without government involvement the poor may be denied access to drugs. Ensuring access to essential drugs, particularly in remote areas, can be a major challenge to those involved in developing and implementing drug policy.

6.2 Drug financing options

Financial sustainability requires a balance between demand, the cost of meeting this demand, and available resources. For example, demand can be changed through improved use of drugs, education, barriers to care and user charges. The cost of meeting the demand can be reduced through improved efficiency and rational use of drugs. Available resources can be increased from patient (co)payments, prepayment (insurance) schemes, government funding from general tax revenue, development loans, endowment funds or donations. Balancing this complex equation is vital for the sustainability of a national drug policy.

Before studying options and choosing strategies, it is helpful to develop a clear picture of the situation and to review some basic information. The government's stand on key policies related to trade, economy and health should be examined. It is also necessary to know how much is currently spent on health and drugs, and whether this is likely to change. What are the relative shares of the private and public sectors? An assessment of the extent to which people have access to essential drugs and a clear description of problems relating to equity and known market failures can be helpful in setting priorities for action.

Improving efficiency and reducing waste

Various measures can be taken to increase value for money and to contain costs at each stage. Rational selection has been discussed in Section 4 and increased affordability in Section 5. Efficient tendering, bulk procurement and improving storage and distribution are discussed in Section 7. Proof that available resources are used wisely and efficiently is a strong argument to justify requests for increased funding.

Increasing government funding

Many countries maintain a commitment to public financing of health services, including essential drugs. Justification for government financing for essential drugs may be strengthened by demonstrating the health impact of drugs, recognizing their social and political importance, showing improved drug management and reduced waste, and presenting solid data to support the drug quantities and budget needed.

In the case of limited public resources for health it is important to carefully (re)define government policy (for example, reconfirming a policy of solidarity) and select priorities for public funding on that basis. Suggested priority areas would be: childhood vaccination services; the prevention and treatment of certain infectious diseases with a high public health impact, such as cholera and tuberculosis; mother and child health services, including safe motherhood; and basic health services for the poor and disadvantaged. Careful analysis of the cost-effectiveness of the various interventions may be needed to guide government decisions on where to spend limited public funds.

The same arguments and identified priorities may be used to justify an increase in government funding. After all, public funding of health care is equivalent to a health insurance system with the largest possible risk pool.

Prepayment schemes and health insurance

Prepayment schemes and health insurance share the risk of health costs between those participating in the scheme. These schemes include compulsory social health insurance, social security, private insurance, managed care (which links health care providers to insurers) and small-scale community health insurance.

The advantages of this approach are that the healthy part of the population also contributes. In this way the total amount of funds available is increased; the health risks are pooled so that care becomes affordable and accessible to more people; and equity shifts are possible (when the rich pay higher premiums than the poor).[35]

In general, a larger pool of participants leads to more robust schemes. In view of the advantages mentioned above, it is recommended that governments back the establishment or expansion of health insurance schemes through supportive legislation and subsidies. WHO provides useful guidance on the design of social insurance schemes.[36,37]

Introducing or increasing user charges

User charges are increasingly being applied by governments and local communities to supplement general government revenues and to help control use of drugs. Often, however, user charge schemes have not been adapted in the light of experience and are not well managed. As a result, the poor and needy are often excluded, revenue replaces rather than supplements government funding, and drugs are often overprescribed.

It is not easy to make these schemes work well. Critical factors in their success have been: local control of revenue; effective and accountable management; constant or increasing levels of government funding; adequate protection or exemption mechanisms to ensure equitable access; reliable supplies of low-cost essential drugs of recognized quality; locally appropriate fee schedules; and phased implementation, beginning in larger hospitals or in some districts.

As user charges charge only the sick and do not generate any revenue from the healthy population, they usually fail to generate enough income for the health system as a whole. User charges are also known to have an anti-equity effect, as the poor are either excluded or pay a disproportionate part of their income for services. For this reason user charges alone cannot be recommended as a sustainable solution.

Development loans

Development loans can contribute to the development of the human and physical infrastructure for the health care system. However, obligatory counterpart contributions to donor-driven projects should not divert scarce public funding away from identified national priorities. Therefore, such investments should be made only when they clearly fit within the national drug policy and within the identified national priorities. It should be cautiously reviewed to finance recurrent costs, which would normally include drug supplies, through development loans.

Donations

Foreign aid can be given to finance the development and implementation of a national drug policy, or to finance the implementation of some parts of the master plan. Donations may also be used to pay for high-priority commodities, such as vaccines or essential drugs for the neediest groups, or for treating diseases with a large public health impact.

Drug donations can save lives and reduce suffering, but only as a temporary measure. Donations do not create a sustainable financing system, and some may actually prevent or delay it. Guidelines for drug donations are discussed in Section 4.2.

7   Supply systems

7.1 Public or private? Or mixed?

Who has responsibility for the supply system, and how it should be structured, are important choices with many political and economic ramifications. It is very important that the drug policy defines the future supply system and the role of the government. There are several options, and which one is chosen will depend on existing structures, the balance between public and private sectors, and other factors.

In some countries problems with the central medical stores and the public supply system have been overcome by contracting some of the work out to private operators while maintaining a centralized structure. For example, the transport of drugs can often be left to the private sector. In other countries different structures are used. An autonomous or semi-autonomous agency is set up to serve as a supply agency not directly managed by the government. The objective of such a system is to combine the efficiency of the private sector with the public health approach and the economies of scale that can be achieved in a centralized system.

Further options include direct delivery systems or primary distributor systems. In a direct delivery system drug prices are established by tender, but drugs are supplied directly to facilities. A primary distributor system is one in which contracts are negotiated with a single prime vendor who supplies and distributes directly to districts or major facilities.[8]

A well-coordinated supply system will ensure that public funds available for drug purchases are used effectively to maximize access, to obtain good value for money and to avoid waste. This will increase confidence in health services and promote attendance by patients. There needs to be good coordination between these central elements of the supply system. Failures at any point of the drug supply system can lead to shortages or to waste. Both the health and the economic consequences can be serious.

The choice of policy on the future drug supply system touches upon many vested interests and discussions on this subject tend to be heated and long. However, it is important for the government to consider all options very carefully and to take an informed decision on long-term policy before embarking on new activities (sometimes with donor funds), such as setting up regional stores.

7.2 Drug procurement

Operational principles for good pharmaceutical procurement

In many countries drug expenditure constitutes a large proportion of health expenditure. Drug procurement is therefore a significant factor in determining total health costs, and it is important to develop a system that helps to ensure efficient procurement for the public sector. However, most of these policies can also be used in the private sector.

WHO, UNICEF, UNFPA and the World Bank have issued an interagency document with 12 operational principles for good pharmaceutical procurement[30] (see Box 6). These principles are based on four strategic objectives:

1. Procure the most cost-effective drugs in the right quantities.
2. Prequalify reliable suppliers of high quality products.
3. Ensure timely delivery.
4. Achieve the lowest possible total cost.

Box 6

Operational principles for good pharmaceutical procurement

Efficient and transparent management

1. Different procurement functions should be separated and performed by different offices or committees.
2. Procurement procedures should be transparent, following formal written procedures.
3. Procurement should be planned, and performance monitored and audited regularly.

Drug selection and quantification

4. Public drug procurement should be limited to a national essential drugs list.
5. Procurement documents should list drugs by their generic name.
6. Order quantities should be based on a reliable estimate of actual need.

Financing and competition

7. Mechanisms should be put in place to assure reliable financing for procurement.
8. Procurement should be done in the largest possible quantities.
9. Public procurement should be based on competitive procurement methods.
10. Members of the purchasing groups should respect supply contracts.

Supplier selection and quality assurance

11. A system of supplier prequalification and monitoring should be in place.
12. Procurement should assure quality according to international standards.

Source: Operational principles for good pharmaceutical procurement. Geneva: World Health Organization; 1999. WHO/EDM//PAR/99.5 (interagency document).

Price information for finished products

Market intelligence is of enormous benefit for drug procurement and strengthens the purchaser's bargaining power. In this regard the *International price indicator guide*[31] presents up-to-date information on the world market price of most essential drugs. Similarly, information on new drugs and their registration status in the country of origin can be valuable. Information on product interchangeability is set out in the guidelines on registration requirements for establishing interchangeability adopted by the WHO Expert Committee on Specifications for Pharmaceutical Preparations.[29] UNICEF, WHO, the Joint United Nations Programme on HIV/AIDS (UNAIDS) and Médecins Sans Frontières (MSF) jointly publish price information on drugs used in the treatment of HIV/AIDS.[38]

7.3 Local manufacture

Policy decisions about whether to import essential drugs from reputable companies or to promote local manufacture, and if so, at what level, should be based on a careful situation analysis and on a realistic appraisal of the feasibility of domestic production.[39] When formulating a policy the most important objective should be to get quality essential drugs to the people who need them, at prices that they and their country can afford.

Pharmaceutical production can be classified into three levels. Primary production includes the manufacture of active pharmaceutical ingredients and intermediates; secondary production includes the production of finished dosage forms from excipients and active substances; and tertiary production is limited to the packaging of finished products or repackaging of bulk finished products.

Make or buy?

Many governments are politically interested in developing or maintaining local manufacturing capacity and in increasing self-reliance. There may be a complex mixture of health and economic arguments to consider. A government may hope to provide a regular supply of low-cost drugs to public health programmes aimed at disease control, through government-owned drug manufacture rather than through local or overseas procurement. Some governments consider that drug manufacturing plants may contribute to reducing foreign exchange needs, provide employment, improve the balance of trade and the viability of the plants through drug exports, and contribute to industrial development and transfer of technology.

In reality, however, these assumptions are rarely justified and the difficulties of establishing or even maintaining a viable and competitive industry should not be underestimated. Any decision about whether a government should be involved in pharmaceutical production and if so, at what level, should be based on a thorough situation analysis to determine the feasibility of any proposals. Particular attention should be paid to the real costs (including the need for highly qualified technical and commercial staff, imported equipment, spare parts and raw materials), and the quality and prices with which the locally produced drugs will compete in the market.

In general, drug and vaccine production is best left to the private sector. The role of the government should move away from owning or managing drug production plants, towards regulation and inspection of drug production by the private sector. The government may promote the quality of locally produced drugs, and thereby strengthen industrial capacity, by arranging for training in GMP.

Price information on raw materials

WHO and the International Trade Centre in Geneva issue a monthly price indicator for pharmaceutical raw materials needed for the production of the most common essential drugs.[40] This service is intended to assist national industries in their market research for the procurement of active ingredients at competitive prices.

7.4 Distribution strategies

Public sector

Whether or not a public sector supply system operates with cost-recovery, decentralized drug budgets, "cash-and-carry" or other systems, it should be well designed and given sufficient human and financial resources to be run properly. The performance of the distribution system defines whether or not patients will receive the essential drugs they need.

As mentioned above, the best systems are probably based on a combination of public and private management. For example, the transport of drugs and supplies can often be done better by private transport companies. In all cases, distribution and storage should be monitored to ensure the quality of drugs at all levels of the distribution network.

Availability of essential drugs in rural areas depends heavily on the distribution system within the districts. In several countries, such as Kenya, Uganda and the United Republic of Tanzania, monthly ration kits have been used. However, they are inflexible and involve higher direct costs. They can also lead to surpluses and shortages of some drugs. If the necessary managerial and administrative structures are in place this "push" system should be changed into a "pull" system on the basis of lists of essential drugs and supplies for rural facilities. A simple requisition system includes the use of a maximum stock at the rural facility (usually set at three months' consumption) towards which monthly orders are placed by rural staff.

Private sector

In most countries the majority of the population is serviced by private-sector drug supply systems, which include private wholesalers, distributors, pharmacists and informal drug sellers. Although growing in most countries, in developing countries the private sector is still concentrated mainly in urban areas and usually fails to serve rural areas fully. When developing a national drug policy it is important to take this sector into account, since it can play a role in maximizing access to health care.

Motivating the private sector to cover less profitable areas of the country may need a system of incentives, such as government subsidies, public or "people's" pharmacies, or franchising. Another approach to increasing access through the private sector is by a programme of training in prescribing for drug sellers (see under rational use). This may require legal changes.

7.5 Drug supply in emergency situations

In times of natural or man-made disasters, the world community is usually quick to send large and often unsolicited donations of drugs and medical supplies. Under these circumstances drug donations can be of great help and can save lives, but some drug donations can do more harm than good. Donated drugs may not be adequate for the emergency, their names may be unknown and their labels in the wrong language. They may arrive unsorted, without clear packing lists. They may be close to their expiry date, or consist of large boxes of drug samples and unused drugs that have been returned to the pharmacy.

Guidelines for drug donations

WHO has collaborated with most international humanitarian emergency relief agencies to obtain the maximum benefit from drug donations. They have developed interagency *Guidelines for drug donations*[17], which are intended as a guide for donors and recipients. The 12 articles of the guidelines are based on the following four core principles:

1. Drug donations should provide for maximum benefit to recipients, and must be based on their needs.

2. Donors should respect the wishes and authority of the recipient country.

3. There should be no double standards in drug quality.

4. Maximum communication between donor and recipient is vital.

The most important practical aspects of the 12 articles are that, as far as possible, drug donations should be based on an expressed need, consist of drugs that are on the list of essential drugs of the recipient country, and have a remaining shelf-life of at least 12 months after arrival in the country.

As part of a national drug policy it is recommended that the government develops and issues national guidelines for drug donations, and communicates these to its main development partners. During an emergency, the government should immediately establish a coordinating body to assess and inform the donors about needs, approve donations, and coordinate their receipt and distribution.

Additional guidelines for donations of single-source (usually patented drugs) are in preparation.[41]

New Emergency Health Kit

Large population movements or a sudden influx of refugees may create an immediate need for basic health services. A large group of international agencies active in humanitarian emergency relief has developed a standard kit of essential drugs, supplies and basic equipment, the *New Emergency Health Kit.*[42] This kit contains all that is needed for basic health care in the first phase of an acute emergency, and is kept ready for dispatch within 24 hours by several international suppliers.

Safe disposal of unwanted pharmaceuticals

Some drug donations are never used and ultimately create an environmental problem. WHO, in collaboration with many other organizations, has issued interagency guidelines for the safe disposal of excess stock or unwanted pharmaceuticals in emergency situations.[43] The document contains many practical recommendations that may also be useful in other situations.

8 Drug regulation

Key policy issues

The drug regulatory authority is the agency that develops and implements most of the legislation and regulations on pharmaceuticals to ensure the quality, safety and efficacy of drugs, and the accuracy of product information. Key policy issues are:

- government commitment to drug regulation, including the need to ensure a sound legal basis and adequate human and financial resources;
- independence and transparency of the drug regulatory authority; relations between the drug regulatory authority and the ministry of health;
- stepwise approach to drug evaluation and registration; definition of current and medium-term registration procedures;
- commitment to good manufacturing practices, inspection and law enforcement;
- access to drug control facilities;
- commitment to regulation of drug promotion;
- regulation of traditional and herbal medicines;
- need and potential for systems of adverse drug reaction monitoring;
- international exchange of information.

8.1 Need for drug regulation and quality assurance

The drug regulatory authority (DRA) is the agency that develops and implements most of the legislation and regulations on pharmaceuticals. Its main task is to ensure the quality, safety and efficacy of drugs, and the accuracy of product information. This is done by making certain that the manufacture, procurement, import, export, distribution, supply and sale of drugs, product promotion and advertising, and clinical trials are carried out according to specified standards. Several of these functions also contribute to efforts to promote rational drug use (see Chapter 9).

Drugs of poor quality can have serious health and economic consequences. There are many ways in which the quality of a drug may be unacceptable or poor. Drugs may not contain the right active ingredients in the quantities stated on the label; they may contain no active ingredient at all, or contain substances that could be harmful. The quality may have deteriorated because of poor storage conditions, contamination or repackaging; or the drug may simply have passed its expiry date.

Apart from the medical consequences of ineffective treatments or toxic effects, money is wasted because of the extra costs to the health care system. Considerable wastage may also occur if drugs are not packaged and stored properly, so that new stocks must be procured. There is also a more general psychological effect. If people do not have confidence in the quality of the drugs they receive, they may lose confidence in the drug policy and the health services as a whole.

In recent years, national and international authorities have recognized the presence of substandard and counterfeit drugs as a growing challenge to those involved in quality assurance. Some of this development is linked to trends towards liberalization and globalization of trade. It is a real challenge for a regulatory control system to prevent the procurement, marketing and use of such drugs. WHO has developed guidelines on measures to combat counterfeit drugs.[44]

8.2 Basic requirements for drug regulation

Drug regulation is a complex task, with many stakeholders and vested interests involved. For this reason there are a number of basic requirements.

Sound legal basis, adequate human and financial resources

A DRA can be effective only if it has a legal basis for all its functions. It must have: sufficient competent administrative and technical staff with the necessary integrity; adequate and sustainable funding; access to external experts and international contacts; access to a quality control laboratory; and a reliable system of law enforcement in the courts. The national drug policy must address all of these factors.

Independence

To maintain public confidence the DRA must operate, and be seen to operate, in an independent, authoritative and impartial manner. It must be funded by the government or by fees collected from industry and clients. However, in the latter case, the DRA must be careful that decisions to grant product registration and licences for establishments are not biased by the need to collect fees from pharmaceutical companies and other clients. Fees levied by the DRA should not be so high that they discourage applications for the registration of essential drugs, and act as a barrier to drug availability and affordability. Provisions should therefore be in place for a reduction of or exemption from registration fees in order to ensure that vital and life-saving drugs are available.

It is also important that drug regulatory functions are separated from drug supply functions and from agencies involved in supply management, in order to maintain independence and ensure that there is no conflict of interest. In some situations the DRA can authorize an independent body to perform functions such as drug evaluation and inspection of manufacturers, to ensure that they comply with GMP.

One important policy decision is where to site the DRA: whether it should be within the ministry of health, or within a technically and managerially independent organization that reports to the minister or should be totally independent. Some of the key policy issues concerning the DRA's independence are presented in Table 3. This shows that an organization (which may include the drug quality control laboratory as well), which is technically and managerially independent but reports directly to the minister of health, can have the advantages of a fully independent agency without most of its disadvantages.

Table 3

Key policy issues on the independence of a drug regulatory agency		
	Potential advantages	**Potential disadvantages**
Part of ministry of health (MoH)	• MoH able to set policies	• Low salaries • Inefficient management • Inflexibility with funds; low fees • Conflict of interest with executive MoH functions (e.g. supply)
Technically and managerially independent, but reports directly to the minister	• Competitive salaries • Realistic fee structure • Fees used to fund DRA and for drug control laboratory • No conflict of interest with executive MoH functions • MoH able to set policies	
Fully independent (privatized)	• Competitive salaries • Realistic fee structure • Fees used to fund DRA and drug control laboratory	• MoH cannot set policies • Dependent on users and registration fees • Risk of DRA being "hijacked" by other stakeholders not supporting national drug policy • Incentive to register too many drugs

Transparency

One of the keys to an honest and accountable DRA is transparency in all its procedures and outcomes for all stakeholders. Transparency and openness help to prevent bias and corruption. Some of the means of achieving transparency in drug regulation are:

■ definition, publication and dissemination of the requirements for information to be submitted to the DRA in support of various types of applications;

■ publication of the criteria that the DRA uses and the procedures it follows when making decisions about applications;

■ publication of the DRA's decisions (regular comprehensive lists of drugs registered, renewals and withdrawals) and of the information upon which these are based; a DRA web site may be a convenient way to achieve this.

8.3 Core elements of drug regulation

The main tasks of a DRA are to ensure the quality, safety and efficacy of drugs (including traditional and herbal medicines), and the appropriateness of product information. These four aspects can be translated into a set of core elements of drug regulation (see Box 7).

Box 7

Core elements of drug regulation

Quality:	Review of quality as part of product registration
	Formulation of norms and standards
	Licensing of facilities and personnel
	Inspection of facilities and products
	Drug quality control
Safety:	Review of safety as part of product registration
	Adverse drug reaction monitoring
	Issue of warnings, recall of products
Efficacy:	Review of efficacy as part of product registration
	Authorization of clinical trials
Information:	Review and approval of product data sheets and labels
	Regulation of advertising and drug promotion

The various core elements are discussed in sections 8.5–8.9, with reference to relevant WHO publications and other materials that provide the necessary technical details.

Building an effective and efficient drug regulatory authority is a long and arduous task that may take years to accomplish, with considerable personnel and financial investment. A stepwise approach is usually recommended. In this respect, WHO's *National drug regulatory legislation: guiding principles for small drug regulatory authorities* is relevant for countries with limited resources.[45] This document and most other relevant materials have been brought together in a compendium of WHO guidelines and related materials, published in two volumes.[46]

8.4 Stepwise approach to drug registration

A drug registration system is a major element of national legislation and regulation, and its administration is one of the key DRA functions. Since it is costly and labour-intensive it is best developed in stages. Various registration procedures require different levels of technical expertise and resources. Countries can use the following procedures in the stepwise development of a drug registration system.

Step 1: Notification procedure

This can be used in countries where the drug registration system is just starting. The procedure involves recording standard information about all the pharmaceutical products offered for sale in a country. A drug register or drug list is produced, but no judgement is made about the products. The procedure does not involve checking whether drugs meet basic safety, efficacy and quality criteria, but it provides a useful basis for developing additional control and improving the registration system. Some countries require registration of a product in the country of origin or in some other specified countries.

Step 2: Basic authorization procedure

Drugs listed in the register are provisionally authorized to remain on sale. However, every new drug that is to be sold requires a licence, which is issued after assessment of efficacy, safety and quality, as well as of the accuracy and completeness of the packaging information. The DRA has various options:

■ It can make its own assessment of the quality, safety and efficacy of the product on the basis of information submitted by the applicant. This must be done for products manufactured in the country.

■ It can use assessment protocols from DRAs in other countries as a basis for making decisions about applications.

■ It can rely on decisions made by DRAs in other countries. For imported products, this can be done by using the WHO Certification Scheme on the Quality of Pharmaceutical Products Moving in International Commerce.[47] This indicates whether the product has been registered, whether the product information has been approved by the DRA of the exporting country, and whether the manufacturer conforms to guidelines for GMP. However, not all DRAs are equally well developed and a certificate can never be more reliable than the authority that issues it.

Step 3: Full registration

This involves detailed evaluation of the data submitted before marketing authorization for a pharmaceutical product is granted. This process will decide the indications for a product's use and whether it can be dispensed with or without a prescription. It also involves post-marketing surveillance and periodic review of registration.

Step 4: Re-evaluation of older drugs

All older drugs are systematically reassessed. This could result in a revocation or non-renewal of the registration if there is new information about the product, for example regarding a serious adverse reaction, or if the product no longer meets the efficacy, safety and quality requirements for registration. Most countries have a limited registration period (usually five years). At the end of the period, an application for renewal of registration has to be submitted if the manufacturer wants to continue marketing the product.

8.5 Quality

The quality of a drug or device is one of the criteria for market approval and is reviewed as part of the registration process. Quality assurance covers all activities aimed at ensuring that consumers and patients receive a product that meets established specifications and standards of quality, safety and efficacy. It concerns both the quality of the products themselves and all the activities and services that may affect quality.

Responsibilities of the various actors

Ensuring drug quality is the responsibility of all those involved – from the production of drugs to distribution and dispensing. Both the public sector and the private sector have their share of responsibilities. Detailed discussion of the various groups' responsibilities is found in the relevant sections – specifically those on storage and distribution in the drug supply management area. The following may serve as an overview of responsibilities:

Manufacturers are responsible for developing and manufacturing a good quality product and should adhere to GMP. They should also document their procedures and activities, to ensure the quality of the product.

The *drug regulatory authority* must ensure that drugs approved for marketing are appropriately evaluated and registered; that manufacturers comply with GMP through licensing and inspection; that the quality of imported drugs is ensured, for example through the WHO Certification Scheme; and that drug quality is maintained in the supply system by ensuring good storage and distribution practices, and monitoring the quality of drugs in the distribution chain.

Those involved in *drug procurement* should ensure that drugs are carefully selected, purchased from reliable sources, inspected at the time of receipt, and stored and transported properly. The necessary laboratory testing must be requested, and mechanisms to report quality defects and a recall procedure must be in place.

Those involved in *distribution and dispensing* must ensure the proper storage of products, and their appropriate handling, packaging and dispensing. They must also inform patients about the correct handling and storage of drugs.

Licensing

A mandatory system of licensing manufacturers, importing agents and distributors is essential to ensure that all products conform to acceptable standards of quality, safety and efficacy. In addition, all premises and practices used to manufacture, store and distribute these products must comply with requirements to ensure continued conformity to standards until products are delivered to the end-user.

Before a formal licensing system can become operative, it is necessary to: adopt a precise definition of the various categories of licence-holders; determine the content and format of licences; detail the criteria on which licence applications will be assessed; and provide guidance to interested parties on the content and format of licence applications, and on the circumstances in which an application for renewal, extension or variation of a licence will be required.

Inspection

Inspection is an important strategy for safeguarding drug quality. It is intended to ensure that all activities in drug manufacture, import, export, distribution, etc. comply with regulatory and quality assurance requirements, as well as with regulations. Inspection requires motivated, well-trained and properly remunerated staff. WHO guidelines on inspection are available, and contain check-lists for inspectors, sample forms, standard formats for reports and many useful references.[48,49]

Good manufacturing practices

Overall quality assurance of drug manufacture, including the proper organization of production and control activities, is essential to ensure good quality. These practices are defined in GMP guidelines.[50] Following GMP standards not only guarantees production quality, but may also save money by reducing the number of substandard batches that must be remanufactured or destroyed.

Information about GMP can be communicated between national regulatory bodies through the use of the WHO Certification Scheme on the Quality of Pharmaceutical Products Moving in International Commerce (see Box 8).[47]

Box 8

The WHO Certification Scheme on the Quality of Pharmaceutical Products Moving in International Commerce

The WHO *Certification Scheme on the Quality of Pharmaceutical Products Moving in International Commerce*[47,51] aims to increase and standardize the exchange of information between regulatory agencies. This is especially relevant for drug importing countries with limited resources for regulatory control. Under the provisions of the Scheme the DRA of the exporting country must provide a certificate that gives the following information:
- A statement that the drug is registered and permitted to be sold in the exporting country, and the date and number of the registration. If the drug is not registered, the reasons must be stated.
- A statement that the product information attached to the certificate is that approved for use in the exporting country.
- Confirmation that the manufacturer's facilities are inspected regularly and that they comply with WHO standards of GMP and quality control.

The Scheme is non-mandatory and depends on the good faith of the competent authorities in exporting countries. A certificate can never be more reliable than the agency that has issued it. A country may join the scheme exclusively as an "importing" (certificate-receiving) country, even if it also exports drugs. The Scheme provides the importing authority with information on the status of a product from the exporting country's DRA. It is intended, however, to strengthen licensing and registration in importing countries, not to replace them. It does not cover the transit and storage conditions that exist once products have been released by the manufacturer. Free sale certificates should not be used, as they do not cover data on government inspections and approved indications.

Quality control

Drug quality control laboratories are responsible for checking, by appropriate testing, whether drugs are of the required quality. The resources and technical capacity to carry out these activities at country level vary enormously, but each DRA should have access to a quality control laboratory, which will also play an important role in the registration process and in the surveillance of the quality of marketed products.

A drug quality control laboratory is costly to establish and to maintain. In general it is recommended that all countries should at least have access to a small laboratory where basic tests can be performed, and that such basic facilities are gradually expanded. It may be that the tests can be done properly and more cost-effectively in an existing institution, such as a university pharmacy department or an independent laboratory. Furthermore, there are international quality control laboratories that can provide drug analyses at fairly reasonable prices. WHO has developed practical guidelines for establishing small and medium-sized testing facilities.[52,53]

As drug quality control laboratories require considerable human and financial resources, they can be established and run by a managerially independent drug regulatory agency. The running costs of both bodies can then be funded from the income from registration fees. This often works well, as registration fees may generate considerable income, while laboratory services usually do not. In manufacturing countries, establishing quality control departments within drug manufacturers and wholesalers/distributors may be a prerequisite for the issue of licences. There should be a high level of control, under the strict supervision of government inspectors and the national drug quality control laboratory.

8.6 Safety

The safety of a drug or medical device is one of the criteria for market approval, and is reviewed as part of the registration process. Adverse drug reaction monitoring, and systems for early warnings and recalls are additional ways of ensuring safety after market approval.

Monitoring of adverse drug reactions

National and international pharmacovigilance systems are needed to collect and evaluate information on adverse drug reactions. However, in countries with limited regulatory capacity, establishing a national pharmacovigilance system may not be a priority. If serious adverse reactions lead to the withdrawal of, or severe restrictions on, a drug in one country, this information is made available through various channels. These include WHO's *Drug Alert* messages, which are sent to all DRAs, and publications from the WHO Collaborating Centre for International Drug Monitoring in Uppsala, Sweden.

Countries should consider whether they have the capacity and resources to establish their own adverse reaction reporting mechanism, and the regulatory capacity to use the information gathered. If they do not, they should consider how they can best use the information that is available internationally.

Warning/recall systems

Whether information is based on data from a national system of adverse drug reaction monitoring or available from international adverse drug reaction reporting systems, national DRAs must consider how they can best use the information. Examples of possible actions include suspension of a drug's market approval, the recall of certain batches, a warning in a national drug bulletin, or a separate warning sent out to a list of institutions and key prescribers.

8.7 Efficacy

The efficacy of a drug or device is one of the criteria for market approval and is reviewed as part of the registration process. Different procedures can be used for different categories of drugs (e.g. generic products or new chemical entities).

Review and approval of products with long-established chemical entities

For products indicated for standard uses and containing established ingredients (such as most generic essential drugs), there is usually no need to re-evaluate the efficacy and safety of the active ingredients. Separate national clinical studies would not normally be required. Emphasis should be put on a review of other factors, for example the presentation, bioavailability (when indicated) and quality of the product, and the accuracy of the accompanying information. Requirements for the submission of documents for product registration, and for the process of registration, are set out in WHO guidelines on drug registration requirements.[54]

Review and approval of products containing new chemical entities

Considerably more extensive information is required to support a marketing application for a new drug substance, in order to provide assurance of efficacy and safety. In particular, detailed accounts are required on chemistry, pharmacological properties, toxicological data, reproductive and teratological studies in animals, and clinical studies. Small regulatory authorities need to adopt caution in licensing newly developed products, because they are unlikely to have the capacity to undertake the multidisciplinary assessment applied to them within large, highly evolved authorities, or to monitor their performance in use through post-marketing surveillance. In general, a small authority with limited resources is best advised to wait until this information has been generated and assessed elsewhere before authorizing such a product for use.

Evaluation of traditional and herbal medicines

Improved use of traditional and herbal medicines can be achieved through adequate regulation[25] and through better evaluation of their safety and efficacy. WHO is involved in efforts to identify and document all published evidence on the pharmacology and clinical use of commonly used traditional and herbal medicines.[24] This information can support efforts to integrate traditional and herbal medicines into national health systems.

Authorization of clinical trials

A DRA may occasionally need to consider an application to conduct a clinical trial of an unregistered drug in the treatment of a condition that has high local prevalence. To allow for this contingency, the registration system should include provision for the importation of the necessary materials, subject to appropriate controls. Such trials should take place only after formal clearance has been obtained from the competent registration authority. Moreover, assurances must be obtained that trials will be conducted in conformity with the principles contained in the World Medical Association's Declaration of Helsinki and the guidelines issued by the Council for International Organizations of Medical Sciences.[55] There is growing awareness that it is unethical to undertake clinical trials in developing of drugs that the participants will never be able to afford to continue after the trials have ended.[56] The revision of the Declaration of Helsinki in 2000 was in part prompted by such concerns.[57] (See also Chapter 10).

8.8 Information and drug promotion

A medicine is a chemical product **plus** information. It is a very important task of the regulatory agency to ensure that drug information is unbiased, correct, updated and easily accessible to prescribers and consumers.

Review and approval of product data sheets and labels

The system of drug evaluation and registration includes the review and approval of the product data sheets and labels. This information is usually disseminated through drug inserts or drug formularies. There is increasing discussion of whether the information that the DRA uses to assess the efficacy and safety of new drugs for market approval should be made accessible to public scrutiny – even if the information is unpublished data which the company may consider as confidential. Many provincial and institutional drug committees would like to use this information for their own decisions on clinical guidelines and essential drugs lists.

Drug promotion

Regulations to control drug promotion and to ensure the quality of information provided are important in promoting more rational use of medicines. National drug policies should therefore include provisions for regulating promotional activities. WHO's *Ethical criteria for medicinal drug promotion*[58] can serve as a basis for developing measures to control drug promotion. The guiding principles are that promotion should be in keeping with national health policies and in compliance with national regulations, as well as meeting voluntary standards where they exist. All promotion-making claims should be reliable, accurate, truthful, informative, balanced, up-to-date, capable of substantiation and in good taste.

Monitoring the quality of promotional activities needs adequate resources and a clear political commitment to enforce the relevant regulations. Possible sanctions include appropriate fines and published retractions of misleading claims in the media in which they were originally made.

8.9 Information exchange with WHO and with other agencies

There are many ways in which drug regulatory authorities can exchange information between themselves or with international bodies such as WHO. These are some of the mechanisms:

- **Drug Safety Alerts:** information issued by WHO in case of serious warnings on quality or safety. Also on http://www.who.int/medicines/organization/qsm/activities/drugsafety/orgqsmalerts.shtml

- **WHO Pharmaceutical Newsletter:** a monthly newsletter issued by WHO with information on regulatory decisions by other regulatory agencies. Also on http://www.who.int/medicines/organization/qsm/activities/drugsafety/orgpharmanews.shtml

- **WHO Drug Information:** a quarterly publication with more general drug-related information, as well as reprints of important documents, such as the WHO Model List of Essential Drugs. Also on http://www.who.int/druginformation/

- **UN Consolidated List of Products whose Consumption and/or Sale have been banned, withdrawn, severely restricted or not approved by Governments.** Issued by the United Nations: this will be made available through the WHO web site: http://www.who.int/medicines

- **WHO Certification Scheme on the Quality of Pharmaceutical Products Moving in International Commerce** (see section 8.5): also on http://www.who.int/medicines/organization/qsm/activities/drugregul/certification/certifscheme.shtml

- **WHODRA web site** (with registered access): http://mednet.who.int/

- **United Nations Office for Drug Control and Crime Prevention** (e.g. list of controlled drugs, international conventions): http://www.undcp.org

- **Electronic discussion groups,** such as E-drug: to subscribe contact: majordomo@usa.healthnet.org In text of message put subscribe e-drug (French and Spanish language versions also available). Also INDICES contact: majordomo@usa.healthnet.org In text of message put: Subscribe indices)

Examples of national web sites are:
Australia: http://www.health.gov.au/tga
Brazil: http://www.saude.gov.br/
Canada: http://www.hc-sc.gc.ca/hpb-dgps/therapeut/
Estonia: http://www.sam.ee/
France: http://agmed.sante.gouv.fr/
Mexico: http://www.ssa.gob.mx/
Netherlands: http://www.cbg-meb.nl/
Peru: http://www.digesa.sld.pe/
South Africa: http://www.health.gov.za/crrp.htm
Spain: http://www.cof.es/bot/
Sweden: http://www.mpa.se/ie_engindex.html
Thailand: http://www.fda.moph.go.th/fdaindex.htm
USA: http://www.fda.gov/default.htm
Also: European Medicines Evaluation Agency: http://www.eudra.org/en_home.htm

9 Rational use of drugs

Key policy issues

The rational use of drugs means that patients receive medicines appropriate to their clinical needs, in doses that meet their individual requirements, for an adequate period of time, and at the lowest cost to them and their community. Irrational drug use by prescribers and consumers is a very complex problem, and calls for the implementation of many different interventions at the same time. Efforts to promote rational drug use should also cover the use of traditional and herbal medicines. Key policy issues are:

- development of evidence-based clinical guidelines, as the basis for training, prescribing, drug utilization review, drug supply and drug reimbursement;
- establishment and support of drugs and therapeutics committees;
- promotion of the concepts of essential drugs, rational drug use and generic prescribing in basic and in-service training of health professionals;
- the need and potential for training of informal drug sellers;
- continuing education and independent, unbiased drug information;
- consumer education, and ways to deliver it;
- financial incentives to promote rational drug use;
- regulatory and managerial strategies to promote rational drug use.

Rational drug use requires that patients receive medications appropriate to their clinical needs, in doses that meet their individual requirements, for an adequate period of time, and at the lowest possible cost to them and their community. Rational drug use promotes quality of care and cost-effective therapy. It helps to ensure that drugs are used only when they are needed, and that people understand what the medicines are for and how to use them.

Policies to promote rational drug use need to address the prescribers, dispensers and consumers of drugs as well as manufacturers and sellers, and traditional healers. All these actors have an important influence on how drugs are used. A variety of strategies and interventions are needed to influence drug use.

9.1 Why is it important to promote rational use?

All drugs, including essential drugs, can be used irrationally. Irrational use is widespread in both developing and industrialized countries; it occurs in public and private sector health facilities and in the home. Many of the gains of efficient selection, procurement and distribution can be lost by irrational prescribing and by lack of adherence to treatment by the patient.

Irrational drug use has both medical and economic consequences. In medical terms, inappropriate treatment may lead to unnecessary suffering and death, to iatrogenic disease and hospital admissions, and to increased antimicrobial resistance. Irrational drug use also decreases public confidence in the health care system and attendance rates of curative and preventive services. Economically, irrational drug use leads to an enormous waste of resources and to unavailability of essential drugs in other areas where they may be needed.

9.2 Challenges

Complexity of the issue

The factors that influence drug use are many and interrelated. Changing complex practices that are embedded in cultural and social beliefs and shaped by knowledge, attitudes, infrastructure and economic interests is very difficult. No single approach is likely to work, and some interventions may produce unintended effects. A combination of strategies tailored to the needs of the different groups and different environments is needed.

Conflicting interests

Policies to promote rational use are often controversial and may be opposed for various reasons. Prescribers, and particularly those who also dispense, may have a financial interest in prescribing more drugs or drugs with the highest profit margins; they may resent any interference with their freedom to prescribe. They may also derive a certain status from prescribing many newly marketed or expensive drugs. Pharmacists and drug sellers have a financial interest in increasing the volume of their business; producers want to increase their sales and their marketing practices may conflict with the goals of rational use. Consumers and prescribers may believe that interventions to encourage rational use are intended to cut costs rather than to improve therapy. It is important to identify and consider all these various interests, which are basic barriers to change.

Lack of independent information

In many countries there is little or no access to regular, up-to-date drug information, and health workers and consumers are almost entirely dependent on commercial sources of information. As a result the prescribers and consumers in most developing countries are poorly informed. Even where prescribers and consumers have access to independent drug bulletins, drug information centres and other sources of information, they are also exposed to a huge volume of commercial information. This information imbalance is a serious constraint on policies to promote the rational use of drugs.

Inappropriate drug promotion

Drugs have a potential not only for benefit but also for harm, and their promotion therefore requires special controls to protect the public. Inappropriate promotion of medicinal drugs remains a problem in both developing and developed countries.

Problems relate to scientific accuracy and balance of information, improper induce-ments to prescribers or dispensers, lack of full product information, misleading presentations by medical representatives, and promotional activities disguised as educational or scientific exercises.

Unrestricted availability of prescription drugs

In many countries medicines that require medical supervision and a prescription are freely available from drug sellers and pharmacies. This can lead to inappropriate use and to delays in the correct diagnosis and treatment. Unrestricted availability can also contribute to the emergence of drug resistance, drug interactions and adverse effects, and inefficient use of scarce household resources.

9.3 Planning for activities to promote rational use of drugs

The problems and potential solutions related to rational drug use are complex. The government should therefore take a leadership role in developing a clear policy on how to promote rational drug use. This policy should lead to a comprehensive national programme to promote rational drug use by health workers and consumers, covering both public and private sectors. Its implementation should be part of the national master plan. The high economic cost of irrational drug use justifies a large investment in budgetary and human resources.

Investigating the problems before interventions are planned

Before any strategies are developed it is essential to identify, measure and understand the problems. There are a variety of tools and methods available which can help in this. The WHO manual *How to investigate drug use in health facilities*[59] presents a useful and simple screening method for identifying and measuring the quality of prescribing and dispensing. This standardized method has been used in over 40 countries and allows for a comparison between countries and regions, and for monitoring the effect of interventions.

Other methods may use aggregated information, combining drug procurement and morbidity data. Investigating practices at retail drug outlets can provide valuable information about private sector practices and consumer behaviour. Standardized methods for studying drug use in the community are also available.[60] Qualitative research methods can then be used to help understand why a problem exists and how it might best be changed. Investigating the nature, scale and cause of a problem is vital because it helps in the choice and design of strategies.

WHO and the International Network for the Rational Use of Drugs (INRUD) organize international training courses on promoting rational drug use, which focus on methods of studying and selecting strategies to improve drug use. The course module can be used and adapted to national needs. A new (2000) WHO international training course specifically focused on public education is also available. The course covers how to study drug use in the community, prioritize problems and select effective channels of intervention.

Combining approaches to achieve maximum impact

It is recommended that a combination of educational, managerial and regulatory strategies is used. The activities should be planned in such a way that they act to reinforce one another. Rules and regulations may exist, but they may have little impact if the target groups are not educated and informed and if management and supervision systems are not in place. Complementary measures and a combination of strategies that work should be identified for different target groups.

Evaluation and selection of approaches

Careful monitoring and evaluation are needed for policy-makers to determine which approaches and strategies work best, or whether strategies may have to be changed. Standardized indicators are available for this purpose. It is also important to recognize that negative outcomes provide useful information as well.

9.4 Core strategies to improve drug use

Strategies to promote rational drug use can be educational, managerial or regulatory. All parties need to be educated and encouraged to use drugs rationally; some managerial measures may help to ensure implementation; and regulations may be needed to enforce some of them, especially for the private sector.

Any strategy and intervention should be focused on a specific problem behaviour, and targeted at the people or facilities with an evident problem. Involving the target group in developing and implementing strategies is important for the success of the intervention.

A few very effective approaches are essential building blocks in efforts to promote rational prescribing.[61] These are the development of clinical guidelines leading to essential drugs lists and formularies, and the establishment of drugs and therapeutics committees in major hospitals. These are discussed first.

Clinical guidelines and essential drugs lists

The starting point for most, if not all, interventions to promote rational drug use is nationally agreed clinical guidelines. These guidelines should cover the most common diseases and complaints, be differentiated for the different levels of health care, and be adapted to the competence of the health workers. Clinical guidelines define the desired prescribing behaviour and constitute the core of all educational, regulatory and managerial interventions. In addition they define the selection of essential drugs for the supply system, as expressed in the various lists of essential drugs.

Clinical guidelines indicate the most cost-effective therapeutic approach, on the basis of valid clinical evidence. Their impact is greatest if the end-users (prescribers and, to a certain extent, patients) are closely involved in the development.

WHO has defined recommended treatments for the most common diseases and complaints. Summaries of these guidelines and references to the full documents are available from the WHO Medicines web site http://www.who.int/medicines/

A variety of printed materials can be used to further promote rational prescribing. Drug bulletins provide summarized, comparative, independent and up-to-date information on selected drugs, and often include information about the cost of treatment. Providing balanced, independent drug information is particularly important in view of the volume of promotional material that is received by prescribers. However, experience has shown that printed information on its own has a limited impact. Printed materials are most useful when used with other, more interactive interventions, such as discussion groups, problem-based learning and prescription review.

Drugs and therapeutics committees

Drugs and therapeutics committees can play an important role in improving the efficiency of the pharmaceutical system, both nationally and at institutional levels. In addition to the national committee to coordinate development of the national clinical guidelines and the national essential drugs list, governments should therefore promote the establishment of such committees in all public and private hospitals.

Hospital drugs and therapeutics committees are vital structures for implementing comprehensive and coordinated rational drug use strategies in hospitals. They should be considered as an organizational keystone in the hospital pharmaceutical programme, which should be responsible for developing and coordinating all hospital policies related to pharmaceuticals (e.g. on the selection of standard treatments, hospital formularies and drug budgets). These committees should also be responsible for adapting the national clinical guidelines and essential drugs list to the needs of the hospital. They should also perform drug utilization studies and prescription reviews, and develop educational strategies to improve drug use and management. A WHO manual on the establishment and functions of drugs and therapeutics committees is being developed.

9.5 Educational strategies

Rational use depends on the knowledge, attitudes and practices of health care practitioners and consumers. Educational strategies for both groups are essential but frequently neglected or inappropriate. In the case of health care practitioners there is often a focus on the transfer of narrow, time-limited pharmacological knowledge, rather than on the development of lifetime prescribing skills and the ability to assess drug information critically.

The education of consumers is a particularly neglected area in all parts of the world. This is of especial concern in developing countries, where prescription products are widely available without prescription from numerous sources, such as pharmacies, grocery stores and market vendors, and where drug promotion is ill-regulated and frequently inappropriate. In some countries up to 80% of medicines are purchased directly by consumers without passing through formal health care channels. Thus an educational strategy that concentrates solely on health care practitioners will have limited impact on the rational use of medicines in the population.

Adequate knowledge does not always lead to appropriate behaviour. For example, when economic incentives exist to prescribe more expensive drugs, education alone will not change the prescribing pattern. Other interventions, such as a change in remuneration structure, will be needed. Moreover, if the local health centre has no drugs, long queues, and unpaid staff while the friendly market vendor is near at hand, more than education is needed to change consumer behaviour. For this reason it is critical to consider and to understand the environment in which drug use takes place when planning educational strategies.

Basic training of health professionals

Improving the basic training of health professionals is an important strategy for achieving rational drug use. The essential drugs concept and its practical application should be included in the curriculum of all health workers. Emphasis needs to be placed on problem-solving techniques, critical appraisal skills and good communication with patients. The WHO *Guide to good prescribing,*[62] available in over 20 languages, is a very successful student manual on the principles of rational prescribing, which has been adopted by developed and developing countries. It is also being used for in-service training of doctors and has been adapted for the training of paramedical prescribers. A teacher's guide is also available.[63]

Those involved in dispensing drugs (pharmacists, pharmacy assistants) also need to be taught the essential drugs concept and the principles of rational use, and these concepts should be included in their curricula. In addition, they should be trained to communicate effectively with patients, to explain the appropriate use of drugs and to answer questions as part of pharmaceutical care. The role of nurses in prescribing and dispensing and in communicating with patients should also be recognized, and nurses should therefore be included in training programmes.

In-service training of health workers

Continuing education, supervisory visits and focused lectures and workshops can be effective in increasing knowledge and changing behaviour. Experience has shown that the impact on behaviour is likely to be maximized if specific prescribing and dispensing behaviour is targeted, if the groups are small, if known experts are involved in the teaching, and if the training is followed up with specific feedback on their actual prescribing. Face-to-face contact between prescribers and dispensers with trained educators is effective but requires considerable human and financial resources.

Training of drug sellers

In countries where there is a shortage of trained pharmacists and pharmacy assistants, prescription drugs are sold by drug sellers with no formal qualifications or training. Basic in-service training could be provided to them. Practical training based on checklists and simple written information can help them to do their job well and to communicate effectively with patients. Some promising results have been reported.[64]

Drug information centres

An underlying factor in many aspects of irrational drug use is the lack of access to independent drug information. Information supplied by the pharmaceutical industry through mailings, visits by drug representatives and industry-sponsored drug formularies is very often the only type of drug information available to prescribers. Drug information centres are an important tool in responding to the need for independent drug information.

Drug information centres can be established and maintained by the government, or linked to a teaching hospital. The latter is the better option when their functions include a 24-hour poison information service. They can also be very effectively run by NGOs, particularly those targeting information to consumers. Some drug information centres have started with one person and a small set of core books, and then expanded as resources and needs permit. Centres often fail when they try to do too much too soon, without clear prioritization and plans for long-term sustainability. More information on drug information centres is available.[65]

Drug bulletins

Drug bulletins are a useful means to disseminate unbiased and updated drug infor-mation to prescribers and consumers. When they are prepared and issued by the regulatory body they tend to be drug-oriented. Drug bulletins issued by teaching institutions or NGOs tend to be more disease-oriented and comparative in nature.

Consumer information and education

Consumer education is an important area, often neglected in developing and imple-menting national drug policy. Most medicine programmes tend to place greater emphasis on the supply of essential drugs to health centres and the training of health care practitioners to prescribe properly than on promoting rational use of medicines by consumers. However, drug use studies show that people commonly use medicines without health practitioners' advice, that their drug use pattern is shaped by their own experiences with medicines, and that they obtain their medicines from various sources, including the informal sector. Given this situation, more attention should be paid to educating consumers on the appropriate use of drugs.

Patients should be given information about the drugs that they are taking. This is important to promote adherence to treatment and achieve the maximum benefit from the treatment. On a wider scale, public education is needed so that people have the skills and knowledge to make informed decisions about how to use drugs (and about when not to use them) and to understand the role of drugs in health care, with their potential benefits and risks. Recent experience in consumer education on drug use can be found in a WHO report.[66]

Interventions directed towards consumers are most relevant if they focus on patterns of irrational drug use that are common, and cover problems that consumers themselves consider to be important. Useful criteria for prioritising problems include: the scale of the problem, the seriousness of health consequences, the costs, and the appropriateness and feasibility of a community intervention.

Principles to guide public education should include the following:

- public education should be included in national drug policies.

- public education should address important drug use issues that consumers should be appropriately informed about.

- public education should encourage informed decision-making and cover basic concepts related to drug action; how to choose when to self-medicate and when to seek medical advice; which conditions do not require medication; how to read a drug label or patient information.

- public education on drugs should recognize and take account of cultural diversity and the influence of social factors.

- NGOs, teachers, professional associations and community groups have an important role to play in public education programmes and should be involved in planning, development and implementation.

- education programmes should have clear and measurable objectives. It should be recognised that to change deep-rooted beliefs and practices requires a sustained effort and a stepwise process which moves from creating awareness, to acquiring knowledge and finally changing behaviour.

Ideally, education programmes should have long-term sustainability. Although short campaigns, especially using the media, may be used to raise awareness they are most unlikely to change behaviour in the long-term or contribute to sustained community empowerment and knowledge. One important and sustainable approach is to incorporate drug use education in school curricula as part of health education at an early age. Another approach is to include modules in adult education classes, such as literacy courses.

Inappropriate self-medication using prescription drugs, which is widely practised in developing countries, can be dangerous to people's health. It also has economic consequences. Self-medication using antibiotics is an example. The public must be educated about this problem.

Medicines approved as being safe for self-medication (non-prescription drugs) are normally used for the prevention or treatment of minor ailments or symptoms that do not justify a medical consultation. Drugs approved for over-the-counter (OTC) sales should be provided with labels and instructions that are accurate, legible and clearly understandable by laypersons. These should include complete information on the contents of the drug, indications for use and for discontinuing use, recommended dosages, warnings about unsafe use or storage, and warnings about drug interactions. This subject is closely linked to effective drug regulation.

9.6 Managerial strategies to promote rational drug use

Managerial strategies are also important in promoting rational use and in discouraging waste. The most important strategies are discussed below. In all cases, a careful analysis of the underlying problem, extensive discussions with all staff involved, a careful introduction, and intensive supervision and follow-up help to ensure maximum impact of the strategies. In some cases, unexpected negative effects may be the result.

Standard treatments, essential drugs lists, dispensing standards

As mentioned in Section 9.4, clinical guidelines should be used to define institutional or national essential drugs lists, and these should be used to guide drug procurement and reimbursement. Adherence to the clinical guidelines should also be promoted by involving the end-users in their development, by introduction and training in their use, through supervision and medical audit. Other possibilities are the introduction of standardized or structured prescription forms, for example for antibiotic prophylaxis, and the use of standardized course-of-therapy packages.

Some managerial interventions do not work. For example, a rule to limit prescriptions to a maximum of three drug items can easily be evaded by writing two prescriptions for one patient; and a rule to have consultants countersign certain expensive prescriptions can be circumvented by pre-signed empty prescription sheets.

Financial incentives

There is very little hard evidence on the impact of financial incentives. On theoretical grounds it can be assumed that the removal of perverse incentives should lead to better prescribing, but unintended effects are very common.

The combination of prescribing and dispensing functions in one professional usually leads to overprescribing, as there is a financial incentive to sell more or more expensive drugs. It is therefore recommended that these two functions are separated as much as possible, except in rural areas where there is insufficient market for separate pharmacies. Such a measure usually meets with strong opposition by dispensing doctors (who may earn a considerable part of their income by selling drugs) and by pharmacists (who may earn a considerable part of their income by selling drugs without prescription). In both cases the total remuneration of these professionals has to be reviewed, and systems of professional fees (consultation fee, dispensing fee) need to be introduced. Similarly, a percentage mark-up for a pharmacist creates an incentive to sell more expensive drugs. A flat dispensing fee, irrespective of the price of the drug, would remove this incentive but may lead to a price increase of the cheaper drugs. Financial incentives should always be planned and evaluated very carefully.

9.7 Regulatory strategies to promote rational drug use

A well-functioning regulatory system that ensures the efficacy, safety and quality of drugs marketed is a prerequisite for policies to promote rational use. There are various regulatory strategies that support educational and managerial strategies to promote rational drug use. Most have already been discussed in Chapter 8.

Evaluation of drugs for market approval and scheduling

The critical evaluation and rational selection of drugs registered for marketing in the country are among the main vehicles for limiting the availability and irrational use of drugs in the private sector. Scheduling decisions about which drugs are available "over-the-counter" to consumers and which are available "on prescription only" are important in determining how drugs are used, provided that they are enforced (which is, unfortunately, very often not the case). Regulations may be used to allow certain types of drugs to be prescribed by trained paramedical workers, such as nurses and midwives.

Drug promotion

Rational use of drugs is dependent upon people understanding that medicines should be used only when needed, for the correct indications and in the required dosage. Drug promotion influences prescribers and consumers, and regulations to control it are vital to increasing rational drug use. The WHO *Ethical criteria for medicinal drug promotion*[56] can be used as a basis for developing such regulations. Promotion should be in line with national health policies, and comply with national regulations and any existing voluntary standards. For further information see Chapter 8.

9.8 Promoting rational drug use in the private sector

Most of the interventions described above apply to the private sector as well. For example, basic training of health workers, drug registration, pricing policies, regulation of pharmaceutical promotion, positive reimbursement lists and public education affect the private sector just as much as the public sector. There are a few interventions that specifically aim at the private sector, and these are briefly described below.

Continuing education

In many countries, unfortunately, most continuing education activities are heavily dependent on the support of pharmaceutical companies, as public funds are usually insufficient. Governments should support efforts by university departments and national professional associations to provide independent continuing education, for example based on the national clinical guidelines. This support could be a financial incentive, or simply making sufficient copies of the national clinical guidelines or other materials available.

Regulatory measures and law enforcement

The government could consider regulatory measures to separate prescribing and dispensing functions, in order to remove a perverse incentive. For example, both dispensing doctors and prescribing pharmacists have a tendency to overprescribe. Generic policies, pricing policies and the dispensing fee structure could be used to encourage the use of essential drugs and promote generic prescribing and substitution. Regulations on the sale of prescription drugs could often be better enforced. In view of the many vested interests, a stepwise approach is recommended.

Health insurance

Drug benefits within health insurance schemes can also have a positive effect on rational prescribing in the private sector. For example, when reimbursement of drug costs is restricted to a positive list and to published clinical guidelines, the patient has a financial incentive to put pressure on the prescriber to stay within the limits of these standards.

10 Research

Key policy issues

Operational research facilitates the implementation, monitoring and evaluation of different aspects of drug policy. It is an essential tool in assessing the impact of the drug policy on national health service systems and delivery; studying the economics of drug supply; identifying problems related to prescribing and dispensing; and understanding the sociocultural aspects of drug use. Key policy issues are:
- the need for operational research in drug access, quality and rational use;
- the need and potential for involvement in clinical drug research and development.

10.1 Introduction

Types of research

There are two categories of research that are of particular importance in the development and implementation of national drug policy. **Operational research** is aimed at better understanding of factors affecting drug use, and identifying the best methods of selecting, procuring, distributing and using drugs. Its results help to identify and implement practical and cost-effective measures, and should underpin management decisions. **Drug research and development** includes a broad range of activities, including research into new drugs, drugs for neglected infectious diseases, new dosage forms and manufacturing processes; basic research in chemistry and molecular biology; and clinical and field trials of drugs and vaccines.

Research as a component of a national drug policy

Operational research facilitates the implementation, monitoring and evaluation of different aspects of drug policy. It is an essential tool in assessing the impact of the drug policy on health service systems and delivery, in studying the economics of drug supply, in identifying problems related to prescribing and dispensing, and in understanding the sociocultural aspects of drug use. It is one of the key ways of identifying which measures work and whether they are being implemented effectively. Operational research is needed at all levels of the health service in both industrialized and developing countries, and should be included in every national drug policy.

On the other hand, the capacity of countries to undertake drug research and development varies enormously. It is important that countries assess their capacity and consider carefully whether they can usefully be involved in drug research and development, and if so, what their priorities should be.

Challenges

Probably the most important challenge is that most health workers and policy-makers, and even many staff members of academic institutions, have no time for operational research and are often not really interested in it. Having an open mind to the results of operational research also implies a critical attitude and a willingness to change. The second challenge is that when operational research is finally done, its results are often not fully used to improve strategies and prepare or adapt action plans. For this reason operational research studies should always be developed and carried out in close collaboration with policy-makers. Governments may need to fund such research, in order to ensure that it is undertaken.

10.2 Strategies to promote research

Research can be promoted and, to a certain extent, directed and coordinated by a variety of means, including scientific and technological competition, intellectual stimulation and financial incentives. Coordinating mechanisms vary in nature: medical or health research councils, scientific research councils, publicly or privately funded national institutes, and international research groups can all contribute to shaping priorities and stimulating research. Also, a move towards integration with health system research is gaining ground and should be viewed as an opportunity to maximize impact.

Operational research

A variety of tools have been developed for operational research on various components of a national drug policy. Examples are standardized indicators for monitoring national policies, standardized indicators and sampling methods for measuring rational drug use in health facilities and in the community.[57,58] Many of these can be adapted for use in different settings. The standard indicators and sampling methods have created a standardized measure for change, and also make comparisons possible between various countries or regions.

Multi-country collaborative research projects can also be a useful approach. Working together, countries can share expertise, compare results and develop common strategies to solve shared problems.

Drug research and development

This is a highly complex area and strategies will vary greatly, depending on a country's level of economic development and its research capacity. Development of a drug is extremely costly, and is mostly done by the pharmaceutical industry.

In most low-income countries it is neither feasible nor cost-effective to carry out drug research and development. However, the national drug policy can also cover areas such as clinical trials and the rights of individuals participating in trials. In any country, clinical trials should be undertaken only when they are necessary and when there are appropriate facilities and regulations to protect participants. They should be organized on the basis of scientific criteria and in accordance with good clinical practice, and be approved by the competent national authority. There is growing awareness that it is unethical to undertake clinical trials in developing drugs that the participants will never be able to afford to continue taking after the trial has ended.[53–55]

In middle-income countries it may be important to develop priorities for research and development that are supportive of the drug policy's goals. For instance, research and development to support generic manufacturing could be considered to be a priority in some countries. In industrialized countries it may be a priority to stimulate research and development in areas of importance to public health, such as developing new drugs for infectious diseases affecting poor populations. It is important to maintain good collaboration and communication between industry and academia while maintaining the independence of academic research.

11 Human resources development

Key policy issues

Human resources development includes the policies and strategies chosen to ensure that there are enough trained and motivated personnel available to implement the components of the national drug policy. Lack of motivation and appropriate expertise has been a decisive factor in the failure to achieve the objectives of a national drug policy. Key policy issues are:

- government responsibility for planning and overseeing the development and training of the human resources needed for the pharmaceutical sector;
- definition of minimum education and training requirements for each category of staff;
- career planning and team building in government service;
- the need for external assistance (national and international).

11.1 Introduction

The need for human resources development

Implementing a national drug policy and achieving its objectives depend on people. They will implement the policy only if they understand its rationale and objectives, when they are trained to do their jobs well, paid adequate wages, and motivated to maintain high standards. Development and implementation of a drug policy require highly qualified and experienced professionals, including policy-makers, doctors, pharmacists, pharmacy technicians, clinical pharmacologists, paramedical staff, economists and researchers. Lack of appropriate expertise has been a decisive factor in the failure of some countries to achieve the objectives of their national drug policy.

Human resources development includes the policies and strategies chosen to ensure that there are enough trained and motivated personnel to implement the national drug policy effectively.

Challenges

Managing human resources well is a complex task and various constraints have to be anticipated and overcome. The major challenges are making sure that the right staff are trained and available, retaining staff, and keeping them motivated and up to date. Common problems include:

- a lack of qualified staff in the pharmaceutical sector to carry out the main tasks necessary for the implementation of different aspects of the drug policy, and especially an overall lack of trained pharmacists and pharmacy assistants in most developing countries;

- difficulties in financing the costs of the necessary personnel in the public sector;

■ trained personnel leaving for better-paid jobs in the private sector or abroad;

■ difficulties in keeping staff motivated and maintaining the quality of their work because of limited career prospects;

■ the need to keep personnel up to date with new developments and to ensure that they maintain their skills.

11.2 Strategies for human resource development

The government should take responsibility for planning and overseeing the development of the necessary human resources. The strategies chosen should realistically reflect the needs and capacity of the country, and an adequate budget should be allocated. Consideration of the following aspects will help to ensure the development of a human resources policy that is supportive of national drug policy implementation.

It is necessary to plan from an early stage and to do so for short-, medium- and longer-term needs. A quantitative analysis of the human resources needed (including a realistic estimate of the attrition rate) may help to set priorities. Financial planning should match the financial resources with priority needs. Good planning and appropriate lead times will help to ensure that a sufficient number of trained people are available. Plans should include a career development policy and measures to retain staff in the service.

Education and training

A national drug policy requires a wide range of skills. Staff at all levels need to be familiar with key policy issues that affect the quality, supply and use of drugs, and should understand the key objectives of the drug policy. For each category of personnel, the nature and extent of their involvement in the policy should be clearly defined. This will make it possible to decide on the orientation and level of training required for each category.

There should be a number of minimum educational and training requirements for each category. For example, personnel and staff involved in specific activities to ensure the quality of drugs should be given adequate training in specific areas of quality assurance. Those involved in the drug supply system should receive training in management, supervision and certain administrative skills that they require.

Health providers in general, and prescribers in particular, should be trained in the principles of rational drug use. Adequate time for training in these areas should be provided both in formal and in continuing education programmes. Collaboration with institutions that can provide continuous and sustained training can be explored.

Pharmacists, pharmacy assistants and prescribing nurses are also in a good position to promote the rational use of drugs, and their roles should receive increased attention. In developing countries, the training and supervision of pharmacists, pharmacy technicians and assistants should be emphasized. The appropriate skills and training needs must be identified first.

Career development and team building

Long-term plans are essential for ensuring a balance between training activities and human resources needs. Career planning is important in helping to recruit personnel for government service and in preventing the loss of staff to the private sector. Continuing education programmes and opportunities to collaborate with others can motivate staff, and help to keep them up to date. In addition, attention must be given to the payment of adequate wages and other incentives to retain staff.

The goals of the drug policy and the importance of the various components must be communicated to all concerned. Staff should be given clear responsibilities and targets, and should be informed of successes and failures through monitoring and evaluation. If they feel that they are part of a team, this will help to maintain a sense of involvement, purpose and motivation.

Collaboration with national institutions

Activities that require specialist expertise – for example, drug evaluation and drug information services – can often be carried out more effectively within universities, training institutions or professional societies than within the health ministries. Collaboration between drug regulatory authorities and universities, research institutions, professional societies and individuals maximizes the use of national expertise and resources. It also builds up a network of people who are knowledgeable and involved in the development and implementation of the drug policy. Outside specialists can fill gaps where national expertise is lacking and can be used in national training programmes to pass on their expertise. When appropriate, professionals can be sent for short training programmes abroad.

12 Monitoring and evaluation

Key policy issues

Monitoring and evaluation are an essential part of a national drug policy, and the necessary provisions need to be included in the policy. Key policy issues are:

- explicit government commitment to the principles of monitoring and evaluation;
- monitoring of the pharmaceutical sector through regular indicator-based surveys;
- independent external evaluation of the impact of the national drug policy on all sectors of the community and the economy.

12.1 Monitoring and evaluation are part of a national drug policy

Monitoring and evaluation are also important elements of the national drug policy, and a monitoring and evaluation system should be set up with the necessary staff and an operating budget. The subject has already been discussed as part of the national drug policy process. Some components which need to be included in the drug policy itself (and in the master plan) are briefly summarized here. More details and references are given in Section 2.4.

Why are monitoring and evaluation important?

A system for monitoring and evaluation is a constructive management tool that enables an ongoing assessment of progress, and contributes to the necessary management decisions. It also provides transparency and accountability, and creates a standard by which comparisons can be made between countries, between areas and over time. All of this may produce the necessary evidence that progress is being made (or not), in order to support the policy in discussions with interested parties and policy-makers.

It is a challenge to create and maintain good systems of monitoring and evaluation. Apart from a lack of time, human resources and budget, there is often a basic lack of understanding of the value of monitoring in the first place, and resistance to objectively or critically reviewing the effects of activities formulated in the master plan.

Monitoring national drug policies

To determine whether adequate progress is being achieved with the various components of the drug policy or the master plan, it is helpful to set realistic targets or performance standards. Indicators can be selected and used to measure progress towards the targets, and to make comparisons over time or between countries and areas. The indicators should be clear, useful, measurable, reliable and valid. Information on indicators for monitoring national drug policies has been given in Section 2.4.

It is recommended that early in the implementation of the national drug policy a baseline survey that covers the whole country is carried out. This baseline can be used as the starting point for setting targets. Baseline surveys in each of the provinces or regions help to involve regional policy-makers and staff, create awareness of problems in the pharmaceutical sector, and may point to regional differences in performance and resources. Repeated regional or national surveys have yielded very useful information in support of managerial or policy decisions.

Periodic evaluations of the national drug policy

The national drug policy as a whole should also be periodically evaluated, preferably every two to three years. Progress can be measured against the initial baseline survey. Independent consultants or professionals from other countries or from WHO may be invited to complement a national evaluation team. Such periodic evaluations should form an integral part of the pharmaceutical master plan, with the necessary resources allocated from the start.

References

1. WHO. Guidelines for developing national drug policies. Geneva: World Health Organization; 1988.

2. WHO. WHO medicines strategy. Framework for action in essential drugs and medicines policy 2002–2003. Geneva: World Health Organization; 2000. WHO/EDM/2000.1.

3. WHO. Contribution to updating the WHO guidelines for developing national drug policies. Report of the WHO Expert Committee on National Drug Policies. Geneva: World Health Organization; 1995. WHO/DAP/95.9.

4. Reich M. Bangladesh pharmaceutical policy and politics. *Health Policy and Planning* 1994; 9(2): 130–143.

5. Lee MB. The politics of pharmaceutical reform: the case of the Philippine National Drug Policy. *International Journal of Health Services* 1994; 4: 477–494.

6. Dag Hammarskjöld Foundation. Making national drug policies a development priority: a strategy paper and six country stories. *Development Dialogue* 1995; 1: 1–256.

7. WHO Medicines web site at: http://www.who.int/medicines

8. Quick JD, Rankin JR, Laing RO, O'Connor RW, Hogerzeil HV, Dukes MNG, Garnett A, editors. Managing Drug Supply. 2nd ed. West Hartford, USA: Kumarian Press; 1997.

9. Brudon-Jakobowicz P, Rainhorn J-D, Reich MR. Indicators for monitoring national drug policies. A practical manual. 2nd ed. Geneva: World Health Organization; 1999. WHO/EDM/PAR/99.3.

10. MSH/RPM. Rapid pharmaceutical management assessment: an indicator-based approach. Washington D.C.: Management Sciences for Health, Rapid Pharmaceutical Management Project; 1995.

11. WHO. Core indicators for monitoring national drug policies. Geneva: World Health Organization. In preparation.

12. Trap B, Chinyanganya F, Hogerzeil HV, Nathoo KJ, Chidarikire A. How to support a national essential drugs programme by repeated surveys of the pharmaceutical sector: the Zimbabwe experience. Geneva: World Health Organization. In print.

13. Brudon-Jakobowicz P. Comparative analysis of national drug policies. EDM Research Series No.25. Geneva: World Health Organization; 1997. WHO/DAP/97.6.

14. WHO. The world drug situation. Geneva: World Health Organization;1988. Second edition in preparation.

15. WHO. The use of essential drugs. Ninth report of the WHO Expert Committee (including the 11th WHO Model List of Essential Drugs). WHO Technical Report Series No.895. Geneva: World Health Organization; 2000. The List is also available on the WHO Medicines web site: http://www.who.int/medicines/edl.html

16. Grimshaw J, Russell IT. Effect of clinical guidelines on medical practice: a systematic overview of rigorous evaluations. *Lancet* 1993; ii: 1317–1322.

17. WHO. Guidelines for drug donations, 2nd ed. Interagency guidelines. Geneva: World Health Organization; 1999. WHO/EDM/PAR/99.4.

18. WHO. The use of common stems in the selection of International Nonproprietary Names (INN) for pharmaceutical substances. Geneva: World Health Organization; 1997. WHO/EDM/QSM/99.6.

19. WHO. Guidelines for the assessment of herbal medicines. WHO Technical Report Series No.863, Annex 11. Geneva: World Health Organization; 1996.

20. WHO. Good manufacturing practices. Supplementary guidelines for the manufacture of herbal medicinal products. WHO Technical Report Series No.863, Annex 8. Geneva: World Health Organization; 1996.

21. WHO. Quality control methods for medicinal plant materials. Geneva: World Health Organization; 1998.

22. WHO. Basic tests for drugs: pharmaceutical substances, medicinal plant materials and dosage forms. Geneva: World Health Organization; 1998.

23. WHO. General guidelines for methodologies on research and evaluation of traditional medicine. Geneva: World Health Organization; 2000. WHO/EDM/TRM/2000.1.

24. WHO. WHO monographs on selected medicinal plants. Volume 1. Geneva: World Health Organization; 1999. (Volumes 2 and 3 in print).

25. WHO. Regulatory situation of herbal medicines: a worldwide review. Geneva: World Health Organization; 1998: WHO/TRM/98.1.

26. Bennett S, Quick JD, Velásquez G. Public–private roles in the pharmaceutical sector. Implications for equitable access and rational drug use. Health Economics and Drugs, EDM Series No.5. Geneva: World Health Organization; 1997. WHO/DAP/97.12.

27. Velásquez G, Boulet P. Globalization and access to drugs. Perspectives on the WTO/TRIPS Agreement. Health Economics and Drugs, EDM Series No.7. Geneva: World Health Organization; 1999. WHO/DAP/98.9 revised.

28. Correa CM. The Uruguay Round and drugs. Geneva: World Health Organization Task Force on Health Economics; 1997. WHO/TFHE/97.1.

29. WHO. Marketing authorization of pharmaceutical products with special reference to multisource (generic) products. A manual for a drug regulatory authority. Regulatory Support Series No.5. Geneva: World Health Organization; 1998. WHO/DMP/RGS/98.5.

30. The Interagency Pharmaceutical Coordination (IPC) Group. Operational principles for good pharmaceutical procurement. Interagency document. Geneva: World Health Organization; 1999. WHO/EDM/PAR/99.5.

31. MSH. International drug price indicator guide. Washington D.C.: Management Sciences for Health; 1999. (Annual publication, in collaboration with WHO).

32. Correa C. Integrating public health concerns into patent legislation in developing countries. Geneva: South Centre; 2000.

33. WHO. Globalization, TRIPS and access to pharmaceuticals. WHO Policy Perspectives on Medicines No.3. Geneva: World Health Organization; 2001. WHO/EDM/2001.2.

34. WHO. Health reform and drug financing. Selected topics. Health Economics and Drugs EDM Series No.6. Geneva: World Health Organization; 1998. WHO/DAP/98.3.

35. WHO. The world health report 2000. Geneva: World Health Organization; 2000.

36. Normad C, Weber A. Social health insurance: a guidebook for planning. Geneva: World Health Organization/International Labour Organisation; 1994. WHO/SHS/NHP/94.3.

37. Bennet S, Creese A, Monash R. Health insurance schemes for people outside formal sector employment. Geneva: World Health Organization; 1998. WHO/ARA/CC/98.1.

38. UNAIDS/UNICEF/MSF/WHO. Essential drugs used in the care of people living with HIV: sources and prices. Geneva/Copenhagen: Joint United Nations Programme on HIV/AIDS, United Nations Children's Fund, Médecins Sans Frontières, World Health Organization; 2000. Also available at: http://www.who.int/medicines/docs/pagespublications/hiv_relatedpub.htm

39. WHO. Establishing or maintaining domestic production of pharmaceuticals in developing countries: advantages and disadvantages. EDM technical briefing paper. Geneva: World Health Organization. In preparation.

40. ITC in collaboration with WHO. *The Market News Service (MNS) for pharmaceutical starting materials/essential drugs.* Geneva: International Trade Centre; monthly edition.

41. WHO. Interagency guidelines for accepting or endorsing donations or discounts of single-source pharmaceuticals. Interagency guidelines. Geneva: World Health Organization. In preparation.

42. WHO. The new emergency health kit. Drugs and medical supplies for 10,000 people for approximately 3 months. 2nd ed. Interagency document. Geneva: World Health Organization; 1998. WHO/DAP/98.10.

43. WHO. Guidelines for the safe disposal of unwanted pharmaceuticals in and after emergencies. Interagency guidelines. Geneva: World Health Organization; 1999. WHO/EDM/PAR/99.2.

44. WHO. Counterfeit drugs: guidelines for the development of measures to combat counterfeit drugs. Geneva: World Health Organization; 1999. WHO/EDM/QSM/99.1.

45. WHO. National drug regulatory legislation: guiding principles for small drug regulatory authorities. WHO Expert Committee on Specifications for Pharmaceutical Preparations. Thirty-fifth Report. WHO Technical Report Series No.885, Annex 8. Geneva: World Health Organization; 1999.

46. WHO. Quality assurance of pharmaceuticals. A compendium of guidelines and related materials, Volume 1. Geneva: World Health Organization; 1997. (Volume 2, 1999).

47. WHO. Certification Scheme on the Quality of Pharmaceutical Products Moving in International Commerce. Geneva: World Health Organization; 1997. WHO/PHARM/82.4, Rev.5.

48. WHO. Provisional guidelines on the inspection of pharmaceutical manufacturers. In: WHO Expert Committee on Specifications for Pharmaceutical Preparations. Thirty-second Report. WHO Technical Report Series No.823, Annex 2. Geneva: World Health Organization; 1992. Also reproduced in Quality assurance of pharmaceuticals. A compendium of guidelines and related materials, Volume 2. Geneva: World Health Organization; 1999.

49. WHO. Guidelines for inspection of drug distribution channels. WHO Expert Committee on Specifications for Pharmaceutical Preparations. Thirty-fifth Report. WHO Technical Report Series No.885, Annex 6. Geneva: World Health Organization; 1999. Also reproduced in Quality assurance of pharmaceuticals. A compendium of guidelines and related materials, Volume 2. Geneva: World Health Organization; 1999.

50. WHO. Good manufacturing practices for pharmaceutical products. WHO Expert Committee on Specifications for Pharmaceutical Preparations. Thirty-second Report. WHO Technical Report Series No. 823, Annex 1. Geneva: World Health Organization; 1992.

51. WHO. Guidelines for implementation of the WHO Certification Scheme on the Quality of Pharmaceutical Products Moving in International Commerce. WHO Expert Committee on Specifications for Pharmaceutical Preparations. Thirty-fourth Report. WHO Technical Report Series No.863, Annex 10. Geneva: World Health Organization; 1996.

52. WHO. National laboratories for drug quality surveillance and control. WHO Expert Committee on Specifications for Pharmaceutical Preparations. Twenty-ninth Report. WHO Technical Report Series No.704, Annex 1. Geneva: World Health Organization; 1984.

53. WHO. Good laboratory practices in governmental drug control laboratories. WHO Expert Committee on Specifications for Pharmaceutical Preparations. Thirtieth Report. WHO Technical Report Series No.748, Annex 1. Geneva: World Health Organization; 1987.

54. WHO. Multisource (generic) pharmaceutical products: guidelines on registration requirements to establish interchangeability. WHO Expert Committee on Specifications for Pharmaceutical Preparations. Thirty-fourth Report. WHO Technical Report Series No.863, Annex 9. Geneva: World Health Organization; 1996. Also reproduced in: Quality assurance of pharmaceuticals. A compendium of guidelines and related materials, Volume 1. Geneva: World Health Organization; 1997.

55. CIOMS/WHO. International ethical guidelines for biomedical research involving human subjects. Geneva: Council for International Organizations of Medical Sciences and World Health Organization; 1993.

56. Tan-Torres Edejer T. North–South research partnerships: the ethics of carrying out research in developing countries. *BMJ* 1999; 319: 438–441.

57. World Medical Association. Declaration of Helsinki. Available at: http://www.wma.net Also reproduced in: WHO Drug Information 2000; 14 (3): 160–162.

58. WHO. Ethical criteria for medicinal drug promotion. Geneva: World Health Organization; 1988.

59. WHO. How to investigate drug use in health facilities. Selected drug use indicators. EDM Research Series No.7. Geneva: World Health Organization; 1993. WHO/DAP/93.1.

60. WHO. How to investigate drug use in communities. EDM Research Series No.2. Geneva: World Health Organization. Revised version in preparation.

61. Laing RO, Hogerzeil HV, Ross-Degnan D. Ten recommendations to improve use of medicines in developing countries. *Health Policy and Planning* 2001; 16(1): 13–20.

62. De Vries TPGM, Henning R, Hogerzeil HV, Fresle DA. Guide to good prescribing. A practical manual. Geneva: World Health Organization; 1994. WHO/DAP/94.11.

63. Hogerzeil HV, Barnes KI, Henning RH, Kocabasoglu YE, Möller H, Smith AJ, Summers RS, de Vries TPGM. Teacher's guide to good prescribing. Geneva: World Health Organization. In print.

64. Kafle KK, Gartoulla RP. Self-medication and its impact on essential drugs schemes in Nepal. A socio-cultural research project. EDM Research Series No.10. Geneva: World Health Organization; 1993. WHO/DAP/93.10.

65. German Foundation for International Development (DSE). Drug information centres in developing countries. In: Report of an international seminar on improving drug information systems in developing countries, 28 May – 3 June 1995. Berlin: DSE; 1995.

66. Fresle D, Wolfheim C. Public education in rational drug use. Geneva: World Health Organization; 1997. WHO/DAP/97.5.